D1234159

BEST OF GREEK CUISINE

Hippocrene is NUMBER ONE in
International Cookbooks

Africa and Oceania
Best of Regional African Cooking
Egyptian Cooking
Good Food from Australia
Traditional South African Cookery
Taste of Eritrea

Asia and Near East
The Best of Taiwanese Cuisine
Imperial Mongolian Cooking
The Joy of Chinese Cooking
The Best of Regional Thai Cuisine
Japanese Home Cooking
Healthy South Indian Cooking
The Indian Spice Kitchen
Best of Goan Cooking
Best of Kashmiri Cooking
Afghan Food & Cookery
The Art of Persian Cooking
The Art of Turkish Cooking
The Art of Uzbek Cooking

Mediterranean
Best of Greek Cuisine
Taste of Malta
A Spanish Family Cookbook
Tastes of North Africa

Western Europe
Art of Dutch Cooking
Best of Austrian Cuisine
A Belgian Cookbook
Cooking in the French Fashion (bilingual)
Celtic Cookbook
Cuisines of Portuguese Encounters
English Royal Cookbook
The Swiss Cookbook
Traditional Recipes from Old England
The Art of Irish Cooking
Feasting Galore Irish-Style
Traditional Food from Scotland
Traditional Food from Wales
The Scottish-Irish Pub and Hearth Cookbook
A Treasury of Italian Cuisine (bilingual)

Scandinavia
Best of Scandinavian Cooking
The Best of Finnish Cooking
The Best of Smorgasbord Cooking
Good Food from Sweden
Tastes and Tales of Norway
Icelandic Food & Cookery

Central Europe
All Along the Danube
All Along the Rhine
Best of Albanian Cooking
Best of Croatian Cooking
Bavarian Cooking
Traditional Bulgarian Cooking
The Best of Czech Cooking
The Best of Slovak Cooking
The Art of Hungarian Cooking
Hungarian Cookbook
Art of Lithuanian Cooking
Polish Heritage Cookery
The Best of Polish Cooking
Old Warsaw Cookbook
Old Polish Traditions
Treasury of Polish Cuisine (bilingual)
Poland's Gourmet Cuisine
The Polish Country Kitchen Cookbook
Taste of Romania
Taste of Latvia

Eastern Europe
The Best of Russian Cooking
Traditional Russian Cuisine (bilingual)
The Best of Ukrainian Cuisine

Americas
A Taste of Quebec
Argentina Cooks
Cooking the Caribbean Way
Mayan Cooking
The Honey Cookbook
The Art of Brazilian Cookery
The Art of South American Cookery
Old Havana Cookbook (bilingual)

BEST OF GREEK CUISINE

Cooking with Georgia

Expanded Edition

Georgia Sarianides

HIPPOCRENE BOOKS, INC.
New York

Expanded paperback edition, 2001
Copyright© 1997, 2001 by Georgia Sarianides
Drawings by CarolJean McFaul-Lopez

All rights reserved.

For information, address:
HIPPOCRENE BOOKS, INC.
171 Madison Avenue
New York, NY 10016

ISBN 0-7818-0883-9

Printed in the United States of America.

Contents

Acknowledgments

A special thanks to my loving husband Peter, and our four children John, George, Despina, and Peter Jr. Today, my son Peter Jr. is my manager. Peter and Despina have worked very hard to help me make my dreams come true. This second edition of *The Best of Greek Cuisine: Cooking With Georgia* is dedicated to them for their great help and support in making it possible. Thank you, Peter and Despina. I would like to wish you both the best of luck with your new company, LS Management.

My thanks and deep love to my parents Margarita and John Liakopoulos, who always taught me to pursue my dreams with confidence and assurance. Thank you for your efforts in my upbringing and for allowing me to play a little and learn a lot in your kitchen—my love to you both forever. Also thanks and love go to my in-laws, Despina and George Sarianides.

My gratitude also goes to my publishing house, Hippocrene Books, Inc., and my editor Carol Chitnis-Gress. Thank you for your hard work.

And last, but certainly not least, I would like to recognize the reader of my cookbook. It is for you that I have compiled the best of the best in cooking and eating—for your pleasure and health. To taste my recipes is to know me. And, if we should cross paths wherever we are, I would be very happy if you would say "Hi Georgia, I love your cookbook." Because I love people and cooking in just that order.

Introduction

I was born and raised in the Peloponnese region, where I had a dream of becoming a chef. Today my dream has become reality. As a child I never even imagined that so many stepping-stones in my life would be crossed. For many years my husband and I owned and operated restaurants in the Massachusetts area. Our four children gave us a helping hand, which afforded me the time to teach the culinary art of Greek American cooking through the media of television and as an adult education teacher. I have not only shared my recipes in this book but also on my Boston TV show, *Cooking With Georgia*, and on national television programs, where I was able to share my love for cooking on a whole different level. I like to think that my book is about not just Greek cooking, but that it also reflects my own personal style in the kitchen.

I hope that those who have never been to Greece will find using my cookbook a very gratifying and surprisingly uncomplicated experience. When the day comes for a trip to Greece, you will have an insight into our eating habits. Wherever you travel in Greece, you will find variations of these recipes that you are about to enjoy.

It is readers like yourself, who love exploring the world of food, that have encouraged me to compile my recipes for your pleasure.

Kali Orexi! (Good Eating!) *Yiasou!*

Georgia Sarianides
Norwood, Massachusetts

Herbs and Spices

Add in small amounts, ¼ teaspoon for each 4 servings. Taste before adding more. Crush dried herbs or snip fresh herbs before using. If substituting fresh for dried, use 3 times more fresh herbs.

Basil: Sweet warm flavor with an aromatic odor, used whole or ground. Good with lamb, fish, roasts, stews, ground beef, vegetables, dressings and omelets.

Bay Leaves: A pungent flavor, use whole leaf but remove before serving. Good in vegetable dishes, fish and seafood, stews and pickles.

Cinnamon: Virtually all the cinnamon sold in the United States is the full-bodied, pungent cassia variety.

Cloves: Famous for their spicy fragrance, these nail-shaped buds are imported from Madagascar and Zanzibar.

Coriander: One of the first herbs known to man, coriander is grown in Morocco, Europe and South America.

Dill: Both seeds and leaves of dill are flavorful. Leaves may be used as a garnish to cook with fish, soup, dressings, potatoes and beans. Leaves or the whole plant may be used to spice dill pickles.

Garlic: Formerly used to ward off evil spirits, flavorful garlic is used widely in French and Italian cooking. Greek chefs use it mostly in roasts and sauces.

Honey: Nectar from the flowers, worked and delivered through the bees, and often used in place of granulated sugar. This thick and sweet syrup has many attributes in its many uses.

Mint: Leaves are aromatic with a cool flavor. Excellent in beverages, fish, cheese, lamb, soup, peas, carrots, and fruit desserts.

Nutmeg: Nutmeg, once sold as a charm, has a warm and spicy flavor. It is tropical in origin.

Olive Oil: Oil from olives imparts a delicate, delicious flavor to foods and makes them more digestible and health giving.

Oregano: Strong aromatic odor, use whole or ground to spice tomato juice, fish, eggs, pizza, omelets, chili, stew, gravy, poultry and vegetables.

Parsley: Best when used fresh but can be used dry; use as garnish or seasoning. Try in fish, omelets, soups, meats, stuffing and mixed greens.

Rosemary: Very aromatic, used fresh or dried. Use to season fish, stuffing, beef, lamb, poultry, onions, eggs and bread.

Saffron: Orange yellow in color, this spice is used to flavor or color foods. Use in soup, chicken, rice and fancy breads.

Sage: Use fresh or dried. The flowers are sometimes used in salads. May be used in tomato juice, fish, fondue, omelets, beef, poultry, stuffing, cheese, spreads, corn-bread and biscuits.

Thyme: This slightly pungent herb, one of the most popular, is grown mainly in France and Spain.

General Food Tips

Broccoli should be firm with dark green leaves. The stems should be firm and the head and stems stored and sealed tightly in a plastic bag and refrigerated for no longer than one week.

Cabbage should have a deep green color and be firm to the touch. Store in a plastic bag and refrigerate for no longer than 2 to 3 weeks.

Carrots should be firm and bright orange in color. Remove the green tops before refrigerating in a tightly closed plastic bag.

Cauliflower is chosen with a very white head and green leaves that hug the white florets. Remove the leaves and store the white part in a sealed, plastic bag for one week.

Chicken is a popular meat that can be prepared in many ways. Because chicken skin contains much fat, you should wash chicken thoroughly and remove the skin. When baking a whole chicken, baste with a mixture of 2 tablespoons of olive oil and the juice of 1 lemon. (Lightly beat together.) This not only gives you a nice brown color but it makes chicken crisp with lots of flavor. The trick is to thoroughly bake or roast the chicken and maintain the juices in the meat by basting often.

Garlic heads should be kept in a cool, dry place. Purchase in small amounts and store for no longer than about 2 months.

Lettuce, Romaine or Boston, should be medium to dark green, and stored in a plastic bag for not longer than one week. Make sure the bag has an air-tight seal.

Olive oil is the oil most frequently used in my recipes. Because I strive for more than just flavor and appearance, it is my concern to offer you a healthful, low-calorie meal whenever possible. The Greek people have used olive oil for many years, even before it became popular with health-conscious people. Greece is known for its groves of olive trees and the many uses for the fruit they bear.

Parsley should be dark, springy and rich green in color. Untie the bunch and trim the bottom stems slightly. Separate all the parsley stems and put them in a plastic bag, unwashed, tightly sealed. Refrigerate.

Peppers called for in this book are sweet bell peppers. Peppers should be dark green in color and firm. They are more fragile than some of the other vegetables. Therefore, seal in a plastic bag and use within a week.

Potatoes should be firm and stored in a cool semi-dark room. Properly stored they hold up to one month.

Scallions should be dark green in color and refrigerated for no more than one week.

Soups are one of the most nourishing and appetizing light dishes. They are wholesome eating and a very good way to start off any meal.

Spinach should be dark green and used as soon as possible. Store in a plastic bag, unwashed, in the refrigerator.

Tomatoes should be firm and red in color. If they are not ripe, put them in a bowl with an apple or in a closed brown paper bag at room temperature. If they are too ripe, refrigerate and use them sliced for garnishing.

Zucchini are best if small to medium in size. They should be firm and dark green. Refrigerate for 4 to 5 days. Skins are usually tender enough to leave on and eat.

Working with Fillo Dough

You can make your own fillo dough from scratch. However, this is a very busy day and age in which we rely heavily on the frozen food department. Make sure to remove your fillo dough from the freezer the day before you intend to use it. It is important that the fillo is kept moist while you are working with it. Keep a moist paper towel over the dough while you are preparing the recipe.

First, butter the bottom of the pan. Then cover the bottom of the pan with leaves of fillo dough and brush with butter. Make sure to keep the rest of the fillo covered as you are working with each piece so that it doesn't dry out. Work quickly, adding layers and brushing each leaf with butter until you have about 15 leaves or more (depending on the requirements of your recipe). Add your filling and cover with fillo layers as in the beginning. Butter the top leaf and sprinkle lightly with water. This will maintain the shape of the fillo dough and keep it from cracking apart. Bake in the oven for the required time in your recipe.

WORKING WITH FILO DOUGH

Wine List Selections

Below you will find a list of Greek wines with detailed descriptions. I would like to suggest that you select one that complements your recipe and that special meal. I guarantee that you will hear raves of delight from your family and guests, and you will have the pleasure of creating a delicious and healthful gourmet meal.

From the Greek wineries and a perfect blend of tastes in harmony with your Greek foods.

NAOUSSA

Origin: Product of the northern Greek vineyards of Naoussa, on the slopes of Mount Vermion, which was the home of Dionysos (or sus), God of Wine.

Variety: 100% Xinomavro, one of the noblest Greek red grape varieties.

Characteristics: One of the most typical Greek V.Q.P.R.D. wines, a classic "vin de garde." It has a bright red color, a spicy aroma with a touch of wood, rich mellow bouquet, full taste and a lingering aftertaste.

Serving Suggestions: A fine accompaniment for roasts and stews, highly spiced dishes, game and cheese.

PAROS

Origin: Product of the Aegean Island of Paros with its picturesque "terraced" vineyards.

Variety: 65% white Monemvasia and 35% red Mandilaria.

Characteristics: This unique combination of the white Monemvasia and red Mandilaria yields a crystal-clear red V.Q.P.R.D. wine, with a fresh aroma of flowers and berries and a smooth balanced taste.

Serving Suggestions: Pleasant on its own, or to accompany light, modern cuisine or cheeses.

GOUMENISSA
Origin: Produced from the vineyards of Goumenissa in Western Macedonia.

Variety: 70% Xinomavro and 30% Negosca.

Characteristics: The union of these two varieties endows this splendid red V.Q.P.R.D. wine with a complex bouquet of spices and ripe fruit, a pleasant mellow taste, full body and long aftertaste.

Serving Suggestions: Accompanies perfectly roast meats and full-flavored cheeses.

KRETIKOS
Origin: From the countryside around Heraklion, Crete, an area rich in Minoan history.

Variety: 70% Vilana, a noble white grape variety.

Characteristics: A smooth white local wine. Its aroma is complex and pronounced, with hints of orange blossom and sweet green apple. Its taste is perfectly balanced, mellow and full, with refreshing aftertaste.

Serving Suggestions: The perfect accompaniment to poultry with white sauces, Chinese dishes, pasta, seafood, fish and fresh salad.

NEMEA
Origin: From the vineyards which surround the ruins of the ancient temple of Zeus, in Nemea in the northeastern Peloponnese.

Variety: 100% Agiorgitiko, the noblest among Greek red grape varieties.

Characteristics: A lively red V.Q.P.R.D. wine with deep red color, rich, ripe, fruity bouquet, velvet-smooth taste, full aroma and delightful lingering aftertaste.

Serving Suggestions: An ideal accompaniment for sausages, cheeses and lightly seasoned red meat dishes.

SANTORINI

Origin: Produced on the island of Santorini, world famous for its volcano, its unique natural beauty, and its archeological treasures.

Variety: 100% Assyrtiko, an exceptional rare Greek white grape variety.

Characteristics: A white V.Q.P.R.D. wine with a personality of its own. Clear yellow in color, its refreshing aroma beautifully blends touches of citrus flowers and ripe fruit.

Serving Suggestions: Perfect with meats in light sauces, fish and seafood.

Soups, Salads & Vegetables

EGG LEMON CHICKEN SOUP
(Kotosoupa Avgolemono)

1 whole chicken (3½ pounds)
1 tablespoon olive oil
¾ cup long-grain rice
2 eggs
juice of 2 lemons
salt and pepper

❑ Wash and trim the excess fat from the chicken. Put the chicken into a large pot and cover with water plus a pinch of salt and bring to a boil. Cover and simmer over medium heat for about 1 hour. Reserve the stock, remove the chicken from the pot and cut it into bite-size pieces. Let the chicken cool and put the pieces into a large bowl. Sprinkle with salt and pepper to taste and cover.

❑ Remove the stock from the pot and add enough water so that it measures 3 quarts of liquid. Strain the liquid through a fine sieve and put it back into the pot. Add the olive oil and bring it to a low boil. Add the rice and stir well. Let it simmer uncovered for another 20 minutes and add more salt and pepper to taste.

❑ Blend the eggs and add the lemon juice while continuously beating. Slowly add one cup hot chicken stock to the egg lemon mixture, while continuing to beat. Add the egg lemon broth mixture to the pan, stirring constantly. Cook over low heat for 2 minutes but do not allow the soup to come to a boil.

❏ Arrange the warm chicken on a platter to accompany the soup; or, put some chicken in each individual bowl.

Makes 6 servings.

BEAN SOUP WITH GREENS
(Pondiaka Fasolia Melahana)

This is one of my favorite recipes, originally from Pondo, Greece, where my father-and mother-in-law lived.

1 pound white navy beans, dry
1 large bunch collard greens
1 large onion, chopped
½ cup olive oil
¼ cup corn flour
salt and pepper
1 lemon sliced (optional)

❑ Soak the beans in a large bowl overnight. The next day, rinse and drain. Put the beans in a medium saucepan and add enough water to completely cover the beans. Boil, uncovered, for 1 hour.

❑ Wash the greens, remove and discard the tough parts. Chop the rest of the greens and add the onion, oil and greens to the beans. Add more water to cover, and salt and pepper to taste and cover. Cook about 30 minutes until the beans are soft. Add the corn flour slowly, while stirring. Cook an additional 15 minutes.

Serve hot. Garnish with lemon if desired.

Makes 6 to 8 servings.

VEAL SOUP WITH VEGETABLES
(Mosxapi Soupa)

4 pounds veal chunks
¼ cup olive oil
1 large onion, chopped
¼ cup red wine
1 can (16 ounces) crushed tomatoes
1 can (16 ounces) artichokes, cut in half
2 carrots, diced
2 large potatoes, diced
2 sticks celery, diced
2 cloves garlic, chopped
1 strip fresh rosemary
1 bay leaf
salt and pepper

❑ Wash and trim fat from the meat and pat dry. In a large pot, heat the oil. Add the onion and sauté lightly. Add the meat and sauté for 10 minutes. Add the wine and stir all together. Add tomatoes with juice, 2½ quarts of water and simmer over medium heat for 45 minutes. Add all the vegetables, the garlic, rosemary, bay leaf, salt and pepper to taste and more water if necessary. Cover and cook for 45 minutes. Remove bay leaf and serve hot.

Serves 8.

LAMB SOUP WITH EGG LEMON SAUCE
(Arni Soupa Augolemono)

A delicious soup that is enjoyed in many Greek homes.

4 to 4½ pounds lamb shoulders or combination
¼ cup olive oil
1 large onion, chopped
¼ cup white wine
3 large potatoes, cubed
2 medium carrots, sliced
3 sticks celery, chopped
salt and pepper
2 large eggs
juice of 1 lemon

❑ Wash and trim the lamb and pat dry. In a large pot, heat the oil. Add the meat and stir for 5 minutes. Add onion and sauté all together for 5 minutes. Add the wine and stir. Add 2½ quarts of water, cover and simmer for 1 hour. Add all the vegetables, salt and pepper to taste and simmer for 35 to 40 minutes. Add more water if necessary. In a blender, beat the eggs 3 minutes. Add the lemon juice and continue beating. Add one cup hot stock slowly while beating to the egg mixture. Beat for 2 minutes. Return the egg mixture back to the pot and over low heat, stir continuously for 2 minutes. Do not let it boil.

Serve hot with crusty bread.

Serves 8.

LENTIL SOUP
(Soupa Faki)

A hearty soup for all seasons.

1 pound of lentils
3 cloves of garlic, chopped
1 onion, chopped
1 green pepper, chopped
3 stalks celery, finely chopped
2 carrots, finely chopped
3 bay leaves
½ teaspoon dried basil
½ teaspoon oregano
½ cup olive oil
1 pound fresh tomatoes, or 1 can (16 ounces)
   crushed tomatoes
salt and pepper
¼ cup red wine vinegar

❑ Wash and sort the lentils. Soak in a pan of water for one hour and drain. Put the lentils into a pot and add fresh water to cover. Boil for 5 minutes. Add the remaining ingredients except tomatoes, salt and pepper and vinegar. Allow mixture to come to a slow boil and simmer for 20 minutes. Add the remaining ingredients. Let the lentils simmer for another hour until the soup is a little thicker.

Serves 8.

MAGIRITZA
A Traditional Easter Soup

1 lamb's organs (liver, heart, tripe and kidney)
¼ cup olive oil
1 large onion, chopped
2 bunches scallions, chopped
½ cup fresh dill, chopped
salt and pepper
1 head romaine lettuce, chopped (4 to 5 pieces)
2 lemons
3 eggs

❑ Wash and drain the organs and put them into a saucepan and add water to cover. Boil for 10 to 15 minutes. Remove from the water and allow them to cool. Cut into medium-size pieces. In a large saucepan, add the oil and organs. Sauté for 2 to 3 minutes. Add onions, scallions, dill, salt and pepper to taste, and 4 to 5 cups of water and cover. Cook for 1 hour on medium heat. Add the lettuce and make sure that the water covers the ingredients and that the pot is stirred occasionally. Simmer for 45 minutes more, making sure that about 2 cups of liquid remain in the pot.

❑ In a blender, process eggs and the lemon juice for a few minutes. Slowly add 1 cup of hot stock to the egg mixture. Continue beating for 2 more minutes. Add the egg mixture to the pan while stirring and lower the heat. Continue stirring while simmering 2 to 3 minutes longer. Do not let this boil.

Makes 4 to 6 servings

BEAN SOUP
(Fasolatha)

This is a healthy soup you'll enjoy.

  1 pound dried white navy beans
  1 large onion, finely chopped
  3 medium carrots, sliced
  2 celery stalks, chopped
  1 can (16 ounces) crushed tomatoes
  2 garlic cloves, chopped
  ½ cup olive oil
  salt and pepper

❑ Wash the beans in cold water and soak them overnight. Rinse them and drain. Put them in a pot completely covered with fresh water. Cover and let boil for 35 minutes. Remove them from the stove and drain off the liquid. Return the beans to the pot and add 3½ quarts of water. Add onions, carrots, celery, tomatoes with juice, garlic and olive oil. Cover and reduce the heat to simmer for 1 hour, add salt and pepper to taste.

Serves 8.

BARLEY SOUP SOURVA
(Pontiakos Sourvas)

This recipe I learned from my mother-in-law. It is one of my favorites.

> 1 pound barley
> ¼ cup olive oil
> 1 large onion, chopped
> salt and pepper
> 1 cup (8 ounces) sour cream

❑ Carefully wash the barley and soak in water overnight. Rinse the barley very well and put in a large pot with enough water to fill it half way. Cover and simmer for 1 hour. In a small saucepan, add the oil, onion, salt and pepper to taste and sauté for 5 minutes. Add the onion to the barley mixture.

❑ Put the sour cream in a medium bowl, and slowly add 1 cup of the hot barley stock while stirring. Add this to the barley soup, stir for 2 to 3 minutes and serve.

Serves 8.

ASPARAGUS
(Salata Me Sparagia)

1 to 2 bunches fresh asparagus (about 1½ pounds)
1 medium onion, grated
½ cup olive oil
juice of 1 lemon
1 teaspoon dried oregano
salt and pepper

❑ Wash and trim the asparagus, and cut into bite-size pieces. Boil in water to cover with a pinch of salt until tender. Remove from pot and drain the asparagus.

❑ Put the asparagus in a bowl and add the onion. In another bowl, mix the oil, lemon juice, oregano, and salt and pepper to taste. Pour the mixture over the salad. Serve cool.

Serves 4 to 6.

CHICKEN SALAD
(Kottosalada)

3 cups cooked and diced chicken breast
1 cup chopped celery
1 medium red pepper, chopped
2 tablespoons fresh chopped parsley
3 tablespoons olive oil
3 tablespoons lemon juice
¾ cup mayonnaise
salt and pepper

❏ In a large salad bowl, combine all the ingredients. Mix well. Chill and serve.

Serves 4 to 6.

CHICORY DANDELION SALAD
(Xopta Salata)

2 bunches dandelion greens or chicory, about 1½
  pounds (store-bought or garden grown)
1 tablespoon salt
¼ cup olive oil
juice of 1 to 2 lemons

❑ Fill a large saucepan halfway with water and bring to a
boil. Wash and rinse your choice of greens making sure
that all dirt is removed. Then, cut the greens in half and
add salt and the greens to the pot of boiling water. Cook
for 40 minutes, pressing down on the greens from time to
time. (This assures that all of the greens will be cooked.)
When the greens are limp and tender, drain the greens and
place them in a salad bowl. Season with olive oil and the
lemon juice to taste.

Serve hot or cold.

Serves 6.

EGGPLANT SALAD
(Melizanosalata)

2 to 3 eggplants
2 cloves garlic, minced
½ cup olive oil
juice of 1 lemon
1 medium onion, grated
¾ cup crumbled feta cheese
salt and pepper
fresh parsley for garnish

❑ Preheat the oven to 375 degrees F.

❑ Wash the eggplants and pat dry. Pierce the eggplants with a fork. Bake them for about 1 hour. Insert a fork to check eggplants for tenderness (they will be soft).

❑ Remove the skin and seeds and process the eggplant in a blender or mixer until it is a smooth pulp. Continue processing and add the garlic, oil, lemon and onion. Sprinkle with salt and pepper to taste and keep processing until the salad mixture becomes very light. Add feta cheese and stir very well.

Serve in a salad bowl and garnish with parsley.

Serves 6.

GARLIC SAUCE
(Skordalia)

This sauce may accompany fish or roasted meat or it may be served as an appetizer.

½ cup olive oil
4 to 5 cloves garlic, crushed
1 pound loaf firm white bread
¼ cup white vinegar
¼ cup fresh parsley, chopped
salt and pepper
black olives for garnish

❑ Cut the crust off the bread, soak in water for 15 minutes, and squeeze out excess. Process the bread in a blender until smooth, then with the blender running, slowly add the garlic, oil, and vinegar until well mixed. Season with salt and pepper to taste and mix for an additional 2 minutes.

Serve the garlic sauce in a salad bowl and garnish with parsley and olives.

Serves 6 to 8 as an appetizer.

GREEK SALAD
(Eliniki Salada)

3 large tomatoes, sliced
2 small cucumbers, sliced
1 medium onion, sliced
1 Italian sweet pepper, sliced
3 to 4 scallions, chopped
1 teaspoon dried oregano
½ cup crumbled feta cheese
5 to 6 black olives
3 tablespoons white vinegar
½ cup olive oil
salt and pepper

❑ Place the vegetables in a large salad bowl in the following order: Tomatoes, cucumbers, onion, peppers and scallions. Sprinkle the oregano, and salt and pepper to taste on the vegetables. Crumble the feta cheese on top and add the olives.

❑ Mix together the oil and vinegar and pour it over the entire mixture of vegetables in the salad bowl.

Serves 4.

GREEK SALAD

GREEK-STYLE POTATO SALAD
(Patatosalata)

6 large potatoes
1 large onion, finely chopped
½ cup fresh parsley, finely chopped
½ cup olive oil
½ cup white vinegar
1½ teaspoon oregano
salt and pepper
3 hard boiled eggs
½ cup black olives

❑ Wash the potatoes very well, leaving the skins on. Put into a large saucepan, and cover completely with water. Boil until they are tender, about 45 minutes to 1 hour, and then drain and cool.

❑ Peel and cut the potatoes into bite-size cubes. Put them into a large salad bowl and add the onion and parsley. Mix together the oil, vinegar, oregano, and salt and pepper to taste and pour mixture over the potatoes. Peel the eggs and cut into wedges.

❑ Garnish salad with the eggs and olives. Serve cold.

Serves 6.

POTATOES WITH GARLIC SAUCE
(skordalia)

5 to 6 russet potatoes
5 garlic cloves, minced
½ cup white vinegar
salt and white pepper
¾ cup olive oil

❑ Peel the potatoes and cover completely with water in a saucepan. Boil until they are tender, about 45 minutes and remove from heat. Drain. Process the potatoes in a food processor with the garlic, vinegar, and salt and pepper to taste. Slowly blend the oil into the mixture, whipping to a creamy smooth. This delicious combination is served warm with fish or any roast as a side dish.

If preferred, sprinkle fresh parsley on top of this sauce for garnish.

Serves 6.

ARTICHOKES WITH EGG LEMON
(Aginares Ayogolemono)

10 large artichokes
juice of 2 lemons
¼ cup olive oil
1 large onion, chopped
½ cup scallions, chopped (1 bunch)
2 large carrots, thinly sliced
½ cup fresh dill, chopped
2 tablespoons fresh parsley, chopped
salt and pepper
2 eggs

❏ Wash the artichokes and remove the outer leaves. Rub them with the juice of 1 lemon and place them into a large bowl. Add 1 teaspoon salt and enough water to cover the artichokes (to prevent them from darkening). Put the oil in the medium saucepan, add the onions and sauté for 3 minutes. Add scallions, carrots, dill, and parsley and sauté for 3 minutes longer. Add 3 cups of water, salt and pepper. Cover and simmer for 15 minutes. Add the artichokes, cover the pot and simmer for 30 minutes. Remove from the stove. Beat the 2 eggs in a blender and add the juice of 1 lemon. Slowly add 1 cup of the hot stock to the egg mixture and then pour it over artichokes. Stir slowly over low heat until sauce thickens.

Serves 4.

BAKED LIMA BEANS
(Fasolia Gigandes)

1 pound dried lima beans
½ cup olive oil
1 large onion, chopped
¼ cup fresh parsley, chopped
3 cloves garlic, crushed
2 large carrots, sliced
1 can (16 ounces) crushed tomatoes
salt and pepper

❑ Wash the beans well and discard any little stones. Soak overnight. Drain. Put the beans into a large pan and cover with water. Let them boil for 1 hour. Remove from the heat. Drain again. Heat the oil in a saucepan and add the onions, parsley, garlic and carrots. Sauté for 5 minutes. Add the tomatoes with their juice and 3 cups of water. Let it simmer for 20 minutes.

❑ Place the drained beans into a baking pan and pour the tomato sauce evenly all over. Add salt and pepper to taste. Stir all together and add 1 cup of water. Bake at 350 degrees F. for 1 hour. They are done when all of the liquid has been absorbed.

Serves 6 as a side dish.

CABBAGE WITH RICE
(Lahanorizo)

This is a delicious vegetarian dish.

1 medium cabbage
½ cup olive oil
1 large onion, chopped
3 cloves garlic, chopped
½ cup fresh parsley, chopped
4 large tomatoes, peeled and crushed
2 bay leaves
1 sprig fresh rosemary
salt and pepper
½ cup rice

❏ Clean and discard any yellow leaves from the cabbage. Remove the core and cut the cabbage in half. Shred cabbage. Put the cabbage into a colander and rinse. Drain. Heat the oil in a large saucepan. Add the onion and garlic and cook until tender. Add the cabbage and parsley. Sauté for 5 minutes. Add the tomatoes, bay leaves, rosemary, salt and pepper to taste and 4 cups of water. Cover and cook on medium heat for 45 minutes.

❏ Add the rice, stirring two to three times. Add 2 more cups of water and stir. Cover the pan and continue to cook the cabbage and rice until they are done (about 1 hour or more). Remove from the heat and cover the pan with a moist towel for 5 minutes, and serve.

Serves 8.

CAULIFLOWER WITH TOMATO SAUCE
(Kounoupithi Kapama)

1 large cauliflower
½ cup olive oil
1 large onion, chopped
2 cloves garlic, chopped
¼ cup fresh dill, chopped
1 can (16 ounces) crushed tomatoes
2 bay leaves
1 sprig fresh rosemary
¼ cup wine vinegar
salt and pepper

❑ Cut off the outer leaves and stem of the cauliflower, and cut into medium pieces, wash and drain. Heat the oil in a pan and fry the cauliflower a few pieces at a time. Transfer the fried cauliflower to a platter. In the same oil , sauté the onion, garlic and dill. Add the tomatoes with their juice, bay leaves and rosemary, and simmer the mixture for 5 minutes. Add the cauliflower and 2 cups of water, vinegar, and salt and pepper to taste. Simmer for about 45 minutes until most of the water has evaporated.

Serves 4 to 6.

FRIED ZUCCHINI
(Tiganita Kolokithakia)

3 to 4 zucchini
salt
1 teaspoon oregano
1 large egg
1 cup milk
1 cup flour
1 cup oil (for frying)
parsley for garnish

❑ Cut off the stems and wash the zucchini. Slice them horizontally and put them into a large bowl. Sprinkle with salt and oregano and let stand for 10 minutes.

❑ In a medium bowl, beat the egg and milk. Dip zucchini in the egg mixture and lightly flour. In a large skillet, add the oil and heat until piping hot. Fry sliced zucchini on both sides until golden brown. Drain them on a paper towel to absorb the excess oil.

Serve hot on a platter garnished with fresh parsley.

Serves 4 to 6 as a side dish.

GREEN BEANS YAHNI
(Fasolakia Yahni)

A delicious vegetarian dish.

1½ to 2 pounds fresh green beans
1 large onion, finely chopped
½ cup olive oil
½ cup fresh parsley, finely chopped
3 cloves garlic, chopped
1 can (16 ounces) crushed tomatoes
salt and pepper

❑ Wash and trim the green beans; string if necessary. Cut or break them in half and wash. Sauté the onion and olive oil in a medium pan. Add the parsley, green beans, and garlic, and sauté 5 minutes more. Add the tomatoes with their juice, salt and pepper to taste, and 3 cups of water; simmer over medium heat for about 1 hour until most of the water has evaporated.

Serves 6.

GREEN PEAS WITH ARTICHOKES
(Aginares Me Arakas)

6 to 8 large fresh artichokes
juice of 1 lemon
salt and pepper
½ cup olive oil
1 large onion, chopped
½ cup fresh dill, finely chopped
½ cup fresh parsley, chopped
1 can (16 ounces) stewed tomatoes
2 pounds fresh or frozen peas

❏ Wash the fresh artichokes and remove their outer leaves. Rub them with the juice of 1 lemon and place them into a large bowl with salt, water and lemon juice so they will not darken.

❏ Heat the oil in a medium pan and add the onion, dill and parsley. Sauté the onion until tender and add the tomatoes plus 2 cups of water. Let simmer for 5 minutes. Add the green peas. Rinse the artichokes and place them on top of the green peas. If necessary, add 1 cup water with salt and pepper to taste. Cover and let simmer over medium heat until most of the water has evaporated (about 45 minutes to 1 hour).

Serve with plenty of bread for dunking and feta cheese.

Serves 6.

PEAS WITH TOMATO SAUCE
(Bizelia)

A delicious vegetarian dish.

½ cup olive oil
1 large onion, chopped
2 pounds frozen peas
½ cup fresh dill, chopped
¼ cup fresh parsley, chopped
1 can (16 ounces) crushed tomatoes
salt and pepper

❑ Heat the oil in a medium saucepan and sauté the onion for 3 minutes. Then add the peas, dill and parsley. Sauté all together for 3 minutes. Add the tomatoes with juice, salt and pepper to taste, and 2 to 3 cups of water. Cover and simmer for 45 minutes, or until the water has evaporated.

Serves 6 as a side dish.

RICE PILAF

This rice pilaf is delicious and may be served as a side dish with any meat of your choice.

¼ cup olive oil
1 large onion, chopped
3 cloves garlic, crushed
2 carrots, chopped
2 cups long grain rice
1 teaspoon dried mint
salt and pepper
4½ to 5 cups chicken broth
¾ cup grated romano cheese

❏ Heat the oil in a medium-size saucepan and add the onion, garlic and carrots. Sauté until tender. Add the rice, stirring contents all together 2 to 3 times. Then add mint, salt and pepper to taste and chicken broth. Stir occasionally and allow the rice to cook on high for 10 minutes. Lower the heat and cover until the liquid is absorbed, about 15 minutes. Add the cheese to the mixture and stir well. Remove from the stove and take off the saucepan cover. Replace it with a damp towel and let it stand for 5 minutes.

Serves 6 to 8.

RICE WITH SPINACH
(Spanakorizo)

A delicious vegetarian dish.

2 packages (10 ounces each) fresh spinach
½ cup olive oil
1 large onion, chopped
1 bunch scallions, chopped
½ cup fresh dill, finely chopped
½ cup fresh parsley, finely chopped
1 can (16 ounces) crushed tomatoes
salt and pepper
½ cup rice

❑ Clean and rinse the spinach leaves two or three times in plenty of water. Cut the leaves into 3 to 4 pieces each. Heat the oil in a medium saucepan and add the onion, scallions, dill and parsley. Sauté until tender. Add the spinach leaves to the pan and toss them a few times until they appear wilted. Add the crushed tomatoes, salt and pepper to taste and 3 cups of water. Cover the pan and simmer for 20 minutes. Add the rice and an additional ½ cup of water and continue stirring. Stir well so that the rice will not stick to the pan. Cover again and let it simmer for an additional 20 minutes. The water will not be completely absorbed by the rice. Remove from the stove and cover the pot with a clean towel.

Let it stand for 10 minutes and then serve.

Serves 6.

BAKED POTATOES WITH GARLIC
(Patates Lathorigano)

6 to 7 baking potatoes
1 tablespoon dried oregano
1 teaspoon dried mint
salt and pepper
½ cup olive oil
juice of 2 lemons
3 cloves crushed garlic

Preheat the oven to 350 degrees F.

❑ Peel the potatoes, wash and quarter them. Put into a medium baking pan and sprinkle with the oregano, mint, and salt and pepper to taste. In a medium bowl, mix the oil, lemon juice and garlic, beat with a fork and pour this mixture over the potatoes and add 2 cups of water. Bake for about 1½ hours until potatoes turn a golden brown. Watch them carefully, if they start to dry out you can add some water midway through the baking time. Remove from the oven and serve hot.

Serves 6.

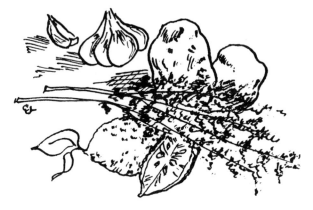

SAUTÉED OKRA
(Mbamies)

2 pounds fresh okra (or 2 packages, 10 ounces
  frozen)
¼ cup white vinegar
½ cup olive oil
1 large onion, finely chopped
3 cloves garlic, chopped
1 tablespoon fresh basil, chopped
1 tablespoon fresh mint, chopped
2 tablespoons fresh parsley, chopped
1 can (16 ounces) crushed tomatoes
salt and pepper

❑ Put the okra into a large bowl and wash, rinse, and drain
well. Carefully cut off and discard the okra stems. Place
the remaining okra into a shallow pan and sprinkle them
with the vinegar. Let it stand for 1 hour.

❑ In a medium pan, heat the oil and sauté the onion, garlic,
basil, mint and parsley until soft. Add the tomatoes and 1
cup of water and simmer for 10 minutes. Add the okra, salt
and pepper to taste and 1 to 2 cups water to cover the okra.
Cover and simmer for 25 to 30 minutes until most of the
water has evaporated. Serve with any kind of roast.

Serves 4 to 6.

STUFFED GRAPE LEAVES WITH RICE
(Dolmathakia Me Rizi)

This side dish makes a delicious appetizer.
The grape leaves can be found at many supermarkets.

1 large jar grape leaves (16 ounces)
¾ cup olive oil
1 cup grated onion
½ cup finely chopped fresh parsley
¼ cup finely chopped fresh mint (or 2 tablespoons
    dried)
2 cups rice
salt and pepper
juice of 2 lemons
lemon slices for garnish

❑ Unfold and rinse the grape leaves very well. Heat half of the oil in a medium saucepan and sauté onions, parsley and mint for 2 to 3 minutes. Add rice and stir for a few more minutes. Add 4 cups of water, and salt and pepper to taste. Lower the heat and cover. Let the rice simmer until all of the water is absorbed, about 10 minutes. Remove from the heat and let it cool.

❑ Spread out one grape leaf at a time and put 1 teaspoon of the filling near the base of the leaf, fold in the sides so that the filling will not fall out, and roll the leaf up tightly. Place the stuffed grape leaves close together in a large saucepan, open side down. Drizzle the remaining oil over them and season with salt. Place a plate on top of the stuffed grape leaves to keep them together while they are cooking. Add enough water to half cover them, and add the juice of the lemons. Cover the pan and bring to a slow boil and simmer for about 1 hour or more. Taste for tenderness.

Garnish with lemon slices and serve.

Serves 3 dozen.

TOMATO OMELET
(Auga Me Tomata)

This is a delicious dish. It is good in the summer for lunch or dinner and is absolutely mouth watering when made with ripe tomatoes from your own garden.

¼ cup olive oil
1 large onion, sliced
3 large fresh tomatoes, chopped and peeled
6 eggs
½ cup kefalotyri or romano cheese, grated
salt and pepper

❑ In a large skillet, heat the oil and sauté onion 3 minutes; add the tomatoes. Simmer for 15 minutes. In a medium-size bowl, beat the eggs with the cheese. Add to the tomato mixture. Stir until the eggs thicken and serve hot.

Serves 4.

Savory Pies

CHICKEN ROLL PIE
(Kotopita)

Can be served as a lunch or dinner.

1½ to 2 pounds chicken breasts
1 cup olive oil, divided
2 large carrots, sliced
1 large green pepper, sliced
1 large onion, sliced
3 cloves garlic, crushed
1 teaspoon dried oregano
salt and pepper
2 large eggs
1 cup crumbled feta cheese
1 pound fillo dough

Preheat the oven to 350 degrees F.

❑ Cut the chicken breasts into long strips. Wash and pat dry. Heat ¼ cup of oil in a large skillet and sauté the chicken strips. Add the carrots, green pepper, onion, garlic, oregano and salt and pepper to taste. Stir all together, then reduce the heat to low. Simmer for 25 minutes and remove from the heat. Let cool for 15 minutes.

❑ Put the chicken mixture into a large bowl. In a smaller bowl, lightly beat the eggs and cheese. Add this to the chicken mixture and combine well.

❑ Using 2 sheets of the fillo dough, brush each thoroughly with oil and stack them. Then take 3 tablespoons of the chicken mixture and place in the middle of one short edge of the dough. Fold end over and both sides in and then roll up into a neat package. Repeat until all of the mixture has been used. Place these rolls on a cookie sheet about one inch apart. Brush olive oil on the tops of each roll and then sprinkle with water to prevent the fillo from cracking. Bake 30 to 40 minutes or until golden brown and serve hot.

Serves 8.

FETA CHEESE BALLS
(Tiropitakia)

This is a great appetizer.

2½ to 3 cups flour
2 teaspoons baking powder
2 sticks melted margarine
1½ cups crumbled feta cheese
¾ cup grated kefalotyri cheese
4 large eggs, divided
1 teaspoon white pepper
1 teaspoon nutmeg

Preheat the oven to 350 degrees F.

❑ Combine flour and baking powder in a large bowl. Make a hole in the center of the flour. Add melted margarine, feta and kefalotyri cheeses and then lightly beat 3 of the eggs into the mixture. Sprinkle with pepper and nutmeg. Blend all together and knead thoroughly until it forms a ball of dough. Let stand for 10 minutes. Grease a cookie sheet. Roll dough into walnut size balls and place on cookie sheet one inch apart. Brush each one with egg and bake for 20 to 25 minutes.

Yields 2 dozen.

GEORGIA'S SPECIAL SPINACH PIE
(Spanakopita)

My delicious spanakopita is a great appetizer.

4 packages (10 ounces each) frozen spinach leaves
1 cup olive oil, divided
1 large onion, finely chopped
1 bunch scallions, chopped
½ cup fresh chopped dill
½ cup fresh chopped parsley
4 large eggs
½ pound crumbled feta cheese
½ cup grated kefalotyri or romano cheese
salt and pepper
1 pound fillo dough

Preheat the oven to 350 degrees F.

❑ Thaw the spinach and squeeze it dry with your hands. Chop into small pieces. Make sure the spinach is thoroughly absent of water. Heat ½ cup olive oil in a medium saucepan. Add the onion, scallions, dill, and the parsley and sauté for 5 minutes. Add the spinach and stir all together. Lower the heat and let simmer for 15 minutes. Take the saucepan off the stove and transfer the mixture to a large bowl. Let cool for 20 minutes.

❑ In a medium bowl, beat the eggs and stir in the feta cheese. Add to the spinach mixture and sprinkle with the kefalotyri cheese, salt and pepper to taste, and mix all the ingredients. Oil the bottom of a medium-size (9 x 13 x 2½ inch) baking pan and line with 8 sheets of the fillo dough, brushing each fillo sheet with oil.

❑ Add the spinach mixture and spread evenly in the pan. Fold any overhanging fillo into the pan. Brush each of the remaining fillo sheets with oil and place on top of the spinach mixture. Trim any excess and brush the top with more oil. Score the top into squares; do not cut all the way down. Sprinkle with water and bake for 35 to 40 minutes. Remove the pie from the oven and let cool. Cut into pieces and serve hot or cold.

Serves 12.

❑ For individual spinach pies, cut the fillo dough into five strips and brush with oil. Put 1 teaspoon of the spinach mixture at one end of the piece of the fillo. Fold up in the shape of a triangle (as you would a flag). Grease a cookie sheet and place pies 1 inch apart. Brush tops with oil. Bake for 15 to 30 minutes.

Makes 3 dozen.

LEEK PIE WITH FILLO DOUGH
(Prasopita)

2 large bunches leeks (about 3 pounds)
1 cup olive oil, divided
¼ cup fresh parsley, chopped
salt and pepper
3 large eggs
2 cups feta cheese, crumbled
½ cup grated parmesan cheese
¼ cup milk
1 pound fillo dough

Preheat the oven to 350 degrees F.

❑ Wash the leeks and remove any yellow leaves. Rinse thoroughly two or three times. Drain and chop into large pieces. Heat ½ cup of the oil in a medium saucepan. Sauté the leeks and parsley together. Add salt and pepper to taste. Simmer on low heat for 10 minutes. Remove the pan from the heat and let it cool for 5 minutes. Combine the eggs, feta, parmesan cheese, and milk in a medium-size bowl. Beat contents slightly. Add this mixture to the leeks and stir all together. Brush a little of the remaining ½ cup oil onto a medium-size (9 x 13 x 2½ inch) baking pan. Put 8 sheets of fillo dough on the oiled pan, brushing each with oil, then pour the leek mixture evenly on the top layer of the fillo dough. Top with the remaining sheets of fillo dough, brushing oil on each one. Trim excess dough with a sharp knife and press down lightly on all sides to secure the filling. Brush the top with oil.

❑ With a sharp knife, mark into 12 squares, but do not cut through the very bottom layer. Bake for 40 to 45 minutes, or until golden brown. Remove from the oven and let them cool for 15 minutes. Fully cut the individual pieces and serve.

You can also serve this pie cold.

Serves 12.

MACARONI PIE WITH FILLO
(Pita Me Makaronia)

This delicious pie can be served with salad for lunch or dinner.

1 package (16 ounces) panoe macaroni
¾ cup margarine, divided
½ cup kefalotyri or parmesan cheese
4 eggs
½ cup milk
1 cup crumbled feta cheese
1 cup (8 ounces) cottage cheese
¼ cup fresh chopped parsley
½ teaspoon nutmeg
salt and pepper
1 pound fillo dough

Preheat the oven to 350 degrees F.

❑ Half fill a large pot with water and add 1 tablespoon salt. Bring to a boil and add the macaroni, whole; do not break into pieces. Boil for 15 minutes and drain. Transfer to a large bowl. Melt half of the margarine in a small pan, pour over the macaroni, sprinkle with kefalotyri or parmesan and mix all together.

❑ In a medium bowl, beat eggs for 3 to 4 minutes. Add milk, feta cheese, cottage cheese, parsley, nutmeg, salt and pepper to taste. Pour the mixture over the macaroni and mix. Grease a 10 x 15 x 2½ inch baking pan and line it with 10 of the fillo sheets; brushing each one with the remaining margarine. Stack them on top of each other in the pan. Spread the macaroni mixture on top of the fillo. Brush each of the remaining fillo with margarine and place them on top of the macaroni. Trim any excess and generously brush the top fillo with margarine. Score the top into squares and sprinkle with some water. Bake for 45 minutes to 1 hour or until the fillo is a golden brown color. Let cool before cutting and serving.

Serves 12.

MEAT PIE WITH FILLO DOUGH
(Kpeatopita)

This pie can be served as a lunch or dinner. Round out the meal with a salad.

¾ cup olive oil, divided
1 large onion, finely chopped
2 cloves garlic, chopped
1 large carrot, chopped
1 large green pepper, chopped
2½ pounds ground beef or lamb
1 teaspoon dried oregano
2 tablespoons fresh parsley, chopped
8 ounce can tomato sauce
salt and pepper
¼ cup dried bread crumbs
1 cup feta cheese, crumbled
2 eggs
1 pound fillo dough

Preheat the oven to 350 degrees F.

❑ Heat ¼ cup oil in a medium-sized pan, add the onion, garlic, carrot and green pepper. Sauté until light brown. Add the ground meat, oregano and parsley, stirring to break up the lumps. Add the tomato sauce and ½ cup of water, salt and pepper to taste. Cover the pan and simmer on medium heat until most of the water is absorbed, about 25 minutes.

❑ Remove the pan from the heat and let it stand for 5 minutes. Add the bread crumbs, feta cheese and lightly beaten eggs; mix well. Lightly oil the bottom of a medium

(9 x 13 x 2½ inch) baking pan and line it with 7 sheets of fillo dough, brushing each fillo leaf with oil as you put it into the pan. Pour the meat mixture over the fillo and distribute it evenly. Fold over any overhanging fillo leaves and brush them with oil. Add remaining sheets of fillo dough on top, brushing oil on each layer. Brush the top with oil. Sprinkle some water over all. Then score with a sharp knife and bake the pie for about 45 minutes to 1 hour. Remove from the oven and let it cool for 20 minutes.

Serves 8 to 10.

HAM ONION PIE
(Kremidopita)

½ cup olive oil
½ pound ham, chopped
5 cups thinly sliced onion
3 cloves garlic, crushed
½ teaspoon dried oregano
½ teaspoon nutmeg
salt and pepper
3 eggs
½ cup milk
1 cup kefalotyri or romano cheese, grated
1 pound fillo dough

Preheat the oven to 350 degrees F.

❑ In a large saucepan, heat the oil and sauté the ham for 1 to 2 minutes. Add the onion, garlic, oregano, nutmeg, and salt and pepper to taste. Stir and cook until the onions are tender, about 15 minutes. Take mixture off the stove and let it cool for 5 minutes. Beat the eggs, milk, and cheese in a medium-size bowl and add this mixture to the onions and mix well.

❑ Oil a medium-size (9 x 13 x 2½ inch) baking pan, and line it with half of the fillo dough. Brush each layer of fillo with oil as you are putting it into the pan. Add the onion mixture to the pan and distribute it evenly. Fold any overhanging fillo into the pan. Brush each of the remaining fillo layers with oil and place them on top of the onion mixture. Trim any excess fillo and generously brush the top layer with oil. Sprinkle with some water. Score the top into squares and bake for 40 to 45 minutes. Let it cool. Cut into complete pieces following the pattern of the scoring.

May be served hot or cold.

Serves 8.

ZUCCHINI PIE WITH FILLO DOUGH
(Kolokithopita)

3½ to 4 pounds medium zucchini
1 cup olive oil, divided
1 large onion, chopped
½ cup fresh chopped parsley
salt and pepper
3 large eggs
1 cup crumbled feta cheese
½ cup grated kefalotyri or parmesan cheese
½ cup cottage cheese
¼ cup farina
1 pound fillo dough

Preheat the oven to 350 degrees F.

❑ Wash and peel the zucchini. Grate and let drain in a colander for 1 hour. Heat ½ cup oil in a medium saucepan, add the onion and parsley, and sauté for 3 minutes. Add the zucchini, salt and pepper to taste, and sauté for 10 minutes. Remove the pan from the heat and set aside for 10 minutes more. In a medium bowl, beat the eggs; add the feta, kefalotyri, and cottage cheese and beat for 2 to 3 minutes. Add the mixture to the zucchini. Sprinkle with the farina and mix all together. Brush a medium-size (9 x 13 x 2½ inch) baking pan with oil. Take 10 fillo sheets, brush each one with oil and place in the pan. Pour the zucchini mixture evenly on the dough. Add the remaining fillo on top, brushing each sheet with the oil. Trim excess dough with a sharp knife. Press down lightly on all sides to secure the filling. Brush top with more oil. With a sharp knife mark into pieces. Do not cut all the way down. Bake for 45 minutes or until golden brown. Let cool for 20 minutes and serve.

Serves 8.

MAIN
Meals

BÉCHAMEL SAUCE

Béchamel sauce is used for mousaka, pasticio and other dishes.

2 sticks butter
1 cup flour
6 cups hot milk
3 large eggs
½ cup kefalotyri cheese or grated romano cheese
½ teaspoon nutmeg

❑ In a medium saucepan, melt the butter and gradually add the flour. Continue stirring for 3 to 4 minutes, adding hot milk and keep stirring for a smooth and creamy consistency. Remove saucepan from the heat.

❑ In a blender, beat the eggs and cheese. With the blender on, slowly add 1 cup of the hot mixture to eggs and beat well for 2 to 3 minutes. Return egg mixture to saucepan and add salt and pepper and nutmeg, stirring constantly. Simmer until mixture is thick and smooth.

Yields 6 to 7 cups.

TZADZIKI CUCUMBER YOGURT DIP
(Tzadziki)

This is a delicious dip served with any roast, and is especially delicious with lamb or souvlaki.

16 ounces plain yogurt
1 large cucumber
½ cup olive oil
1 tablespoon white vinegar
salt to taste
3 cloves garlic, crushed
parsley for garnish, optional

❏ Line a strainer with a towel or coffee filter. Place yogurt in strainer and allow to drain for 3 to 4 hours. Peel, seed and grate the cucumber. Drain on towels.

❏ Combine all of the ingredients in a salad bowl and mix well. Refrigerate before serving.

❏ Garnish with chopped parsley if desired.

Makes 2 cups

CHICKEN WITH GREEN BEANS
(Kota Me Fasolakia)

The flavor of the beans, combined with the chicken, will delight your palate.

1 chicken, 3½ to 4 pounds
¼ cup olive oil
1 large onion, chopped
2 cloves garlic, crushed
¼ cup white wine
salt and pepper
1 can (16 ounces) crushed tomatoes
1½ pounds fresh string beans
¼ cup fresh chopped parsley

❑ Trim the excess fat from chicken. Cut into pieces. Wash, pat dry and set aside. In a medium saucepan, heat the oil and sauté the onion and garlic for 2-3 minutes until soft. Add the chicken and sauté for 10 minutes more. Add the wine, salt and pepper to taste and stir. Add the tomatoes and 3 cups of water, cover and simmer for 45 minutes. Trim the beans, wash and cut in half and set aside. Remove the chicken and place it in a large bowl and cover. Add 2 more cups of water to the remaining sauce and let boil for 2 to 3 minutes. Add the green beans to the sauce and cook for 35 to 40 minutes or until tender, adding more water if necessary. Add the chicken on top of the beans and cook for an additional 15 minutes. Sprinkle with parsley, remove from the heat and let stand for 5 minutes before serving.

Serves 6.

BARBECUED CHICKEN
(Kota Sti Sxara)

Barbecuing has become a year-round addition to everybody's cooking. Whether you barbecue inside or outside, the result is always delicious.

1 chicken, 3¼ to 4 pounds
1 tablespoon dried oregano
1 tablespoon garlic, crushed
1 teaspoon dried thyme
2 bay leaves
½ cup olive oil
juice of 2 lemons
salt and pepper

❑ Cut the chicken into halves and wash and pat dry. Put the chicken halves into a large bowl, mix together the remaining ingredients, and pour marinade over the chicken. Allow 3 hours for chicken to marinate in the refrigerator.

❑ Place the chicken on a hot barbecue grill and baste occasionally on both sides with the marinade. Grill until done, about 1 hour total. Discard any remaining marinade and do not apply to cooked chicken.

Serves 6.

CHICKEN WITH LEMON AND OREGANO
(Kota Ladorigano)

A nice easy dish to enjoy with greens, mashed potatoes or rice.

1 chicken, 4 to 4½ pounds
salt and pepper
½ cup olive oil
3 garlic cloves, crushed
1 tablespoon dried oregano
2 sprigs fresh rosemary
juice of 2 lemons

❑ Wash the chicken, cut into serving-size pieces and drain. Season with salt and pepper to taste. Heat the oil in a large saucepan, add garlic, chicken, oregano and rosemary and sauté until pieces are golden brown on both sides. Add the lemon juice, stirring the chicken to blend the flavors. Add more salt and pepper if desired, and 1 cup of water. Lower heat to medium, cover and let it cook until all water boils away and the chicken is nice and tender, about 1 hour.

Serves 6.

OVEN ROASTED CHICKEN AND POTATOES
(Kota Psiti Sto Fourno Me Patates)

1 chicken, 4½ pounds
2 lemons
4 to 5 cloves garlic, crushed
1 tablespoon oregano
salt and pepper
6 large potatoes
2 bay leaves
1 teaspoon dried thyme
½ cup olive oil
lemon slices for garnish
parsley sprigs for garnish

Preheat the oven to 350 degrees F.

❏ Trim the excess fat from the chicken. Wash and drain. Place the chicken into a large, deep roasting pan. Pour the juice of 1 lemon over the chicken and sprinkle the chicken with half of the garlic, half of the oregano, and salt and pepper to taste. Wash, peel and quarter the potatoes. Place the potatoes in a large bowl and douse with the juice of 1 lemon. Sprinkle with the remaining garlic and oregano, the bay leaves, thyme, and salt and pepper to taste. Place the potatoes around the chicken in the baking pan and drizzle the oil over the chicken and potatoes. Add 2 cups of water to the pan. Bake for about 1½ hours, or until the chicken and potatoes are golden brown. Add more water, if necessary. During the baking process, keep moist by basting the chicken and potatoes occasionally.

❑ Serve the chicken on a platter surrounded with the potatoes and garnished with lemon slices and sprigs of parsley. Delicious with a Greek salad!

Serves 8.

CHICKEN WITH PEAS CASSEROLE
(Kota Me Bizelia)

This delicious casserole has a thick sauce that is wonderful for dunking bread.

1 chicken, 3½ to 4 pounds
salt and pepper
¼ cup olive oil
1 medium onion, chopped
2 cloves garlic, chopped
1 can stewed tomatoes (16 ounces)
2 packages frozen peas (10 ounces each)
½ cup fresh dill, chopped
1/4 cup parsley, chopped

❑ Wash and drain the chicken. Cut into serving-size portions and sprinkle with salt and pepper to taste. Heat the oil in a large pan and sauté the onion and garlic together. Add the chicken pieces and continue sautéing until tender. Add the tomatoes to the pan plus 3 cups of water. Let it simmer for 45 minutes. Wash the peas. Add them to the chicken along with the dill, parsley, and salt and pepper to taste. Cover the let simmer until most of the water evaporates, about 25 minutes.

Serves 6.

CHICKEN BREAST SOUVLAKI
(Souvlaki Me Kotta)

This dish is delicious served with rice pilaf and Tzadziki sauce. See pages 43 and 69.

2 pounds boneless chicken breast
1 teaspoon dried oregano
1 teaspoon dried rosemary
1 juice of lemon
3 cloves garlic, crushed
¼ cup white wine
¼ cup olive oil
salt and pepper
skewers

❑ Wash the chicken and pat dry. Cut into cubes. Place the chicken in a large bowl. Mix the remaining ingredients in a small bowl and pour over the chicken pieces, cover and let stand in the refrigerator for 1 hour. Put 6 to 7 pieces on each skewer and grill or broil 15 minutes on each side. Baste often during cooking. Serve hot.

Serves 4.

CHICKEN KAPAMA WITH TOMATO SAUCE
(Kota Kapama)

Serve hot with rice or pasta, and a delicious Greek salad.

1 chicken, 3½ to 4 pounds
¼ cup olive oil
1 large onion, chopped
2 cloves garlic, chopped
1 can (16 ounces) crushed tomatoes
¼ cup dry white wine
2 cinnamon sticks
2 whole cloves
2 bay leaves
salt and pepper

❑ Wash and cut the chicken into pieces. Heat the oil in a large pot and sauté the onion and garlic for 3 minutes. Add the chicken and sauté 10 more minutes. Add the wine, tomatoes with the juice, cinnamon, cloves, bay leaves, and salt and pepper to taste. Add 2 cups of water, cover and simmer for 1 hour or until the chicken is tender.

Serves 6.

CHICKEN YIOUVETSI
(Yiouvetsi Kotopoulo)

1 chicken, 3½ to 4 pounds
salt and pepper
¼ cup olive oil
1 large onion, finely chopped
2 cloves garlic, chopped
¼ cup white wine
1 (16 ounces) can crushed tomatoes
1 package orzo (16 ounces)
¾ cup kefalotyri or grated romano cheese

Preheat the oven to 350 degrees F.

❑ Trim the excess fat off the chicken. Wash and quarter the chicken. Sprinkle with salt and pepper to taste. Heat the oil in a medium pan and sauté the onion and garlic for 3 minutes. Add the chicken pieces and sauté until golden brown. Add the wine, tomatoes with juice, salt and pepper to taste, and 3 cups of water. Simmer for 1 hour.

❑ Remove the chicken from the pan and place it on a platter. Cover. Put the sauce from the chicken in a medium baking pan and add 4 cups of water. Put the baking pan into the oven and bring the liquid to a boil. Add the orzo and return the pan to the oven. Stir it occasionally and check for dryness. Add more water if necessary. Bake for approximately 30 minutes. Add the pieces of chicken on top of the orzo in the baking pan and bake for about 5 minutes more.

❑ Serve hot sprinkled with kefalotyri or romano cheese.

Serves 4 to 6.

STUFFED CHICKEN
(Kota Yemisti)

Serve this delicious dish with any type of salad or greens; also, rice pilaf.

1 large oven roast chicken, 5 to 6 pounds
½ cup olive oil, divided
1 large onion, finely chopped
3 cloves garlic, crushed
2 tablespoons fresh parsley, chopped
1½ pounds lean ground beef
½ cup white wine
½ teaspoon cinnamon
½ teaspoon nutmeg
salt and pepper
1 (8 ounce) can tomato sauce
1 cup pine nuts (pignoli nuts)
¼ cup dried bread crumbs
½ cup grated romano cheese
1 teaspoon dried oregano
juice of 1 lemon

Preheat the oven to 350 degrees F.

❑ Wash and trim the excess fat from the chicken. Drain. Heat ¼ cup of olive oil in a pan and add the onion and garlic and sauté together for 5 minutes. Add the parsley and the ground beef and stir. Add the wine, cinnamon, nutmeg, and salt and pepper to taste. Simmer for about 5 minutes. Add the tomato sauce and ½ cup of water. Cover and let simmer until most of the liquid is absorbed, 15 minutes.

Remove the pan from the stove and add the pine nuts, bread crumbs, and cheese and mix well.

❑ Sprinkle salt and pepper inside the chicken. Fill the cavity with the stuffing. Close the cavity and place chicken in a medium-sized baking pan. Add the remaining oil. Sprinkle the chicken with the oregano and lemon juice and add 1 cup of water. Add salt and pepper to taste. Bake the chicken for about 1½ hours. Continue to baste the chicken during the baking time. Add liquid to the pan if needed. When the chicken has finished baking, remove from the oven and let it stand for 10 minutes to cool. Open the chicken carefully and remove the stuffing. Place the stuffing in the center of the serving platter and arrange pieces of the cut up chicken around it.

Serves 8.

STUFFED CHICKEN

STUFFED TURKEY
(Galopoula Yemisti)

1 turkey (12 to 15 pounds)
salt and pepper
juice of 1 lemon
1 teaspoon of dried oregano, divided
½ cup olive oil, divided
1 large onion, chopped
2 cloves garlic, crushed
2 pounds lean ground beef
¼ cup white wine
1 cinnamon stick
2 to 3 whole cloves (additional for cavity)
1 teaspoon dried basil
1 can (8 ounces) tomato juice
½ cup rice
1 cup pine pignoli nuts

Preheat the oven to 350 degrees F.

❑ Wash and trim the excess fat from inside the cavity of the turkey and drain. Sprinkle with salt and pepper. Drizzle the lemon juice and sprinkle some of the oregano on the outside of the turkey.

❑ For the Stuffing: Put the oil in a medium pan and sauté the onion and garlic until light brown. Add the ground beef and stir 3 to 4 minutes. Add the wine slowly together with the cinnamon, cloves, oregano, basil and salt and pepper to taste. Add tomato juice and 1 cup of water. Cover and let simmer about 10 minutes. Lower the heat and add the rice. Cover and simmer until all of the liquid is absorbed, about 15 minutes. Remove from the stove. Remove cinnamon stick and cloves and add the pignoli nuts. Let stuffing cool and then fill the turkey cavity with the stuffing. Close the cavity with string. Place the turkey in a baking pan and drizzle it with oil. Add 1 cup of water. Bake for 3½ to 4 hours or until a meat thermometer registers 190 degrees F, basting when necessary.

Serves 10 to 12.

BEEF CASSEROLE WITH PEAS
(Mosyari me Mbezelia)

4 to 4½ pounds beef chunks
½ cup olive oil
1 large onion, chopped
2 cloves garlic, chopped
½ cup red wine
1 (16 ounce) can crushed tomatoes
salt and pepper
2 packages frozen peas, (16 ounces each)
¼ cup fresh parsley, chopped
½ cup fresh dill, chopped
2 large carrots, sliced

Preheat the oven to 350 degrees F.

❑ Wash and pat dry the meat. Heat the oil in a large saucepan and sauté the onions, garlic and meat until lightly brown. Add the wine, and while you are still stirring, add the tomatoes, salt and pepper to taste, and 2 cups of water. Cover and let simmer on low heat for 20 minutes. Remove from the heat. Place meat in a deep baking dish, with the sauce plus 2 cups of water. Bake for 40 minutes more. Then add the peas, parsley, dill and carrots. Season with salt and pepper to taste and stir all together. Add more water when and if necessary. Bake for another 35 to 40 minutes. Remove from the oven and let stand for 5 minutes.

❑ Serve this delicious dish by placing the meat in the center and surrounding it with the peas and other vegetables.

Serves 8.

BEEFTEKI

A delicious barbecued patty with a flavorful lemon topping.

1½ pounds extra lean ground beef
1 large onion, grated
¼ cup chopped fresh parsley
1 teaspoon dried oregano
¼ cup plain dried bread crumbs
salt and pepper
½ cup lemon juice
¼ cup olive oil

❑ In a large bowl, mix the beef, onion, parsley, oregano and bread crumbs. Add salt and pepper to taste. Mix everything very well with your hands. Make into 2-inch patties.

❑ In a small bowl, beat the lemon juice and oil. Preheat the grill. Baste the tops of the patties with the lemon and oil mixture. When one side is done, turn the patties over and repeat the process.

Serves 4.

ONION STEW
(Stufado)

A delicious stew to be served with a hard crusty bread for dipping into the sauce.

  3½ to 4 pounds stew beef
  ¼ cup olive oil
  1 pound small whole white onions
  1 (16 ounce) can crushed tomatoes
  5 cloves whole garlic
  2 sticks cinnamon
  3 bay leaves
  3 whole cloves
  1 sprig fresh rosemary
  ¼ cup red wine vinegar
  salt and pepper

❏ Cut the beef into large chunks. Wash and pat dry. Heat the oil in a large pot. Sauté the pieces until light brown. Add the onions and sauté with the meat for 5 minutes . Add the tomatoes, garlic, cinnamon, bay leaves, cloves, rosemary, and salt and pepper to taste. Add 3 cups water, then add the vinegar. Cover and simmer on medium heat for 1¼ hours until the sauce thickens.

Serves 8.

STUFFED GRAPE LEAVES
(Dolmathakia)

Stuffed grape leaves are good served as an appetizer or with any meal.

2½ pounds lean ground beef
1 large onion, grated
½ cup fresh chopped parsley
1 tablespoon dried mint
¼ cup fresh chopped dill
1 large egg
½ cup rice, uncooked
1 (16 ounces) jar of grape leaves
salt and pepper
¼ cup olive oil
1 lemon for garnish

❑ In a large bowl, combine the meat, onion, parsley, mint, dill, egg, and rice and mix thoroughly. Set aside for 10 minutes. Rinse and drain the grape leaves and trim the tough stems. In a medium saucepan, place 5 large leaves to cover the bottom of the pan. Take 1 tablespoon of the stuffing and place it at the base of each leaf. Fold in the sides and roll up. Place rolls close together in layers in the saucepan. Add salt and pepper to taste. Brush with olive oil and add enough water to cover.

❑ Place a plate over rolls, cover and simmer for 1 hour or until all the water has evaporated. Serve on a large platter garnished with slices of lemon. Good hot or cool as an appetizer.

Serves 8.

STUFFED PEPPERS
(Peppergies Gemistes)

Delicious during the summer with fresh garden peppers.

10 medium peppers
¼ cup olive oil
1 large onion, chopped
2 cloves garlic, crushed
¼ cup fresh chopped parsley
1 tablespoon dried mint
2 pounds lean ground beef
¼ cup wine
¼ cup rice, uncooked
1 can (16 ounces) crushed tomatoes
salt and pepper
1 cup grated parmesan

Preheat the oven to 350 degrees F.

❑ Wash the peppers and cut off the tops. Remove the seeds and set the peppers aside in a 9 x 13 x 2½ inch baking pan. In a medium saucepan, heat the oil and add the onion, garlic, parsley and mint, and sauté 3 minutes. Add the meat and sauté until brown. Add the wine and rice and stir occasionally. Add the tomatoes with juice, salt and pepper to taste and ½ cup of water. Lower the heat and simmer for 30 minutes. Remove from the heat and allow to cool for 5 minutes. Add ½ cup of the cheese and mix well. With a tablespoon, fill each pepper. Sprinkle remaining ½ cup of cheese on top of the peppers. Add 1 cup of water to the bottom of the baking pan. Bake for 1 hour.

Serves 6.

SPAGHETTI WITH MEAT SAUCE
(Makaronia Me Kima)

This is a very tasty dish that is quick and easy to make.

¼ cup olive oil
1 medium onion, chopped
1 tablespoon fresh chopped basil
1 tablespoon fresh chopped mint
2 cloves garlic, chopped
2 pounds lean ground beef
salt and pepper
1 stick cinnamon
2 bay leaves
1 (16 ounce) can crushed tomatoes
16 ounces spaghetti
¾ cup grated kefalotyri cheese

❑ Heat the oil in a saucepan and add the onion, basil, mint, and garlic. Sauté 3 minutes. Add the ground meat and stir until it is well cooked, about 5 minutes. Add salt and pepper to taste, cinnamon, bay leaves, the crushed tomatoes and 1 cup of water. Reduce the heat to medium and simmer for about 30 minutes or until most of the liquid is absorbed.

❑ Bring a large pot of water to a rolling boil. Add 1 tablespoon salt. Add the pasta and cook according to package directions. Remove the cinnamon and bay leaves from the sauce. Drain pasta and place in large shallow bowl; sprinkle with the cheese, then cover the pasta with a thick layer of meat sauce. Sprinkle additional cheese on top.

Serves 5 to 6.

SPICED BEEF WITH TOMATO SAUCE
(Mosxari Kokinisto)

Serve this dish with any pasta, or rice if you prefer.

3½ to 4 pounds lean beef chunks
¼ cup olive oil
1 large onion, chopped
2 cloves garlic, crushed
½ cup white wine
1 can (16 ounces) crushed tomatoes
1 slice orange rind, fresh or dry
3 whole cloves
1 cinnamon stick
salt and pepper

❑ Wash the meat pieces and pat them dry. Heat the oil in a medium saucepan and sauté the onion, meat and garlic together. Stir for 5 minutes on medium heat and add the wine. Stir and add the tomatoes with their juice, orange rind, cloves, cinnamon stick, and salt and pepper to taste. After adding 3 cups of water, cover and simmer for 1 hour or more until sauce thickens. Remove cloves and cinnamon stick before serving.

Serves 6.

STUFFED POT ROAST WITH FETA CHEESE
(Mosxari Gemisto Stin Katsarola)

4½ to 5 pounds beef eye of round
1 teaspoon dried oregano
salt and pepper
2 tablespoons chopped fresh parsley
4 garlic cloves, crushed
1¼ cups sliced fresh mushrooms
½ pound feta cheese
½ cup olive oil
¼ cup white wine
1 can (16 ounces) tomato sauce

❏ Cut open the beef, horizontally, and wash it. Pat it dry and sprinkle with the oregano, salt and pepper to taste, and then spread the parsley, garlic and mushrooms over the opened beef. Slice the feta cheese and place the slices over the other ingredients. Roll up the meat and tie it with string in 4 or 5 places.

❏ Put the oil in a large, deep pot and lightly brown meat on all sides. Add the wine. When most of the wine has evaporated, add the tomato sauce plus 2 cups of water. Cover the pot and simmer on top of the stove, on medium heat, for 1 hour and 45 minutes. Frequently check the meat for liquid and add water when needed. Remove the roast from the pot and place on a large platter. Slice meat and spread the remaining sauce on top.

Serve hot with rice, mashed potatoes or pasta.

Serves 6.

BAKED ZUCCHINI WITH BÉCHAMEL SAUCE
(Mousaka Me Kolokithakia)

béchamel sauce, see page 68
3½ pounds large zucchini
salt and pepper
1 cup vegetable oil
1 cup flour
¼ cup olive oil
1 medium onion, finely chopped
2 cloves garlic, crushed
1 tablespoon fresh chopped mint
2 pounds ground lamb or beef
1 can (16 ounces) crushed tomatoes
1½ cups grated kefalotyri or romano cheese

❑ Preheat the oven to 350 degrees F.

❑ Peel and wash the zucchini and cut in 1 inch slices. Spread out the slices on a large platter and sprinkle them lightly with 1 teaspoon of salt. Heat the vegetable oil in a large frying pan. Lightly flour the zucchini and shake off any excess flour. Fry on both sides until lightly browned. Drain on a paper towel.

❑ Heat the ¼ cup olive oil in a medium saucepan and add the onion, garlic and mint. Sauté until tender. Add the ground meat and cook until brown. Add salt and pepper to taste and the tomatoes with juice. Cover the pot and let it simmer over medium heat for 15 to 20 minutes, or until most of the water has evaporated. Take the mixture off the stove and add half of the cheese and stir well. Grease a medium size (9 x 13 x 2½ inch) baking pan. Spread half of the zucchini slices on the bottom of the pan and sprinkle them with some of the remaining cheese. Cover with an even layer of the meat mixture. Layer the remaining zucchini slices on top of the meat mixture and sprinkle them with all of the remaining cheese. Spread the béchamel sauce over the layer of zucchini.

❏ Bake for 1 hour or until the top takes on a light brown color. Remove the pan from the oven and let it cool before cutting.

Serves 8.

GREEK LASAGNA
(Pasticio)

1 package pasticio pasta (ziti or pene pasta may be
  substituted)
½ cup margarine
3 egg whites
2½ cups grated kefalotyri cheese
¼ cup olive oil plus additional for the pan
1 large onion, grated
3 cloves garlic, crushed
1 tablespoon fresh mint, chopped
1 tablespoon fresh basil, chopped
2½ pounds lean ground beef or lamb
½ cup white wine
1 can (16 ounces) crushed tomatoes
1 stick cinnamon
2 whole cloves
salt and pepper
¼ cup dried bread crumbs
béchamel sauce, see page 68
Preheat the oven to 350 degrees F.

❑ Fill a large pot with water. Add 1 tablespoon salt and bring
to a boil. Add the pasta and boil for only 15 minutes. Drain
and put pasta into a large bowl. Melt the margarine in a
small pan and pour it over the pasta. Lightly beat the egg
whites and pour over the pasta. Using your hands, blend
together the pasta and egg whites plus ¾ cup of the cheese.

❑ Put the oil into a medium pan and add the onion, garlic,
mint and basil. Sauté until tender. Add the ground meat
and sauté lightly. Stir constantly to break up all the lumps.

Slowly add the wine, crushed tomatoes with juice and ½ cup of water. Add the cinnamon, cloves, salt and pepper to taste. Simmer for 20 minutes or until most of the water has evaporated. Take the pan off the stove and mix in ½ cup cheese and the bread crumbs. Remove the cinnamon stick and cloves and stir the mixture well.

❏ Prepare the béchamel sauce. Butter a baking pan, 10 x 15 x 2½ inches, and sprinkle the bottom with half of the remaining cheese. Arrange half of the pasta mixture in the pan. Spread the meat mixture on top of the pasta. Arrange the remaining pasta on top of the ground meat in the same direction as before. Pour the béchamel sauce over the top layer of pasta and sprinkle it with rest of cheese. Bake for 1 hour. As soon as the top is golden brown, remove. Let it cool before cutting.

Serves 8.

Pasticio macaroni may be purchased at any Greek market.

GREEK SPICED MEATBALLS
(Keftethakia)

Delicious anytime as an appetizer.

½ loaf day old, firm bread
2½ pounds lamb, beef or pork
1 egg
1 teaspoon dried oregano
2 tablespoons fresh chopped basil
1 teaspoon dry mint
1 large onion, grated
¼ cup fresh chopped parsley
3 cloves garlic, crushed
salt and pepper
1 cup flour
¾ cup frying oil

❑ Remove the crust from the bread and soak in water for 10 minutes, then squeeze out excess. Put the meat into a large bowl with bread, egg, oregano, basil, mint, onion, parsley, garlic, and salt and pepper to taste. Knead the ingredients well by hand, cover, and refrigerate for 1 hour. Shape small quantities of the mixture into balls, then flour, shaking off the excess. Heat the oil in a medium frying pan and add the meatballs. Cook them thoroughly on all sides. Serve the meatballs on a large platter and garnish with sprigs of parsley. They may be served hot or cold.

Yields 2 dozen meatballs.

GREEK SAUSAGE ROLLS IN TOMATO SAUCE
(Soudzoukakia)

2½ to 3 pounds lean ground beef or lamb
½ cup dried bread crumbs
1 large egg
1 large onion, grated
3 cloves garlic, crushed
1 teaspoon dried oregano
¼ cup fresh chopped parsley
salt and pepper

❏ In a large bowl, mix the beef or lamb, bread crumbs, egg, onion, garlic, oregano and parsley and refrigerate for 30 minutes. Shape 2 tablespoons of the mixture with your hands into rolls about 3 inches long. Place on a broiler pan and broil on both sides until browned. Set aside.

Tomato Sauce:
1 (16 ounces) can tomato sauce
1 stick cinnamon
2 cloves
1 bay leaf
2 tablespoons olive oil
salt and pepper

❏ In a saucepan, simmer all ingredients plus 2 cups water for 25 minutes over medium heat. Add sausage rolls, cover, reduce hea and simmer for 15 minutes more. Serve hot.

Serves 6.

MEATBALLS IN EGG LEMON SAUCE
(Yiouvarelakia Avgolemono)

2½ pounds lean ground lamb or beef
½ cup long grain rice, uncooked
1 large onion, finely chopped
¼ cup fresh parsley, finely chopped
¼ cup fresh dill, finely chopped
3 eggs
salt and pepper
¼ cup olive oil
juice of 1 or 2 lemons

❑ Combine the ground meat, rice, onion, parsley, dill, 1 egg, and salt and pepper to taste in a large bowl. Knead until all the ingredients are mixed well.

❑ Add olive oil to 7 cups of water in a medium-size pot and bring to a boil. Add the meatballs along with a sprinkle of salt and pepper to taste. Then reduce the soup to a low boil over medium heat and continue cooking for 40 to 45 minutes. Add water if necessary. Beat the remaining 2 eggs in a blender. Add the lemon juice. While continuously beating, slowly add 1 cup of hot broth from the pot to the egg mixture. While stirrring, pour the egg mixture back into the pot.

❑ Simmer over low heat until the stock thickens, while being very careful not to boil.

Serves 6.

MEATLOAF ROLL STUFFED WITH EGGS
(Rolo Gemisto Me Auga)

4 hard boiled eggs
2¼ pounds lean ground beef or lamb
1 raw egg
1 large onion, grated
¼ cup finely chopped fresh parsley
2 tablespoons finely chopped fresh mint
1 tablespoon dried oregano
3 cloves garlic, crushed
¾ cup dried bread crumbs
salt and pepper
¼ cup olive oil

Preheat the oven to 350 degrees F.

❏ Peel the hard boiled eggs and set aside. Put the meat and raw egg in a large bowl. Add the onion, parsley, mint, oregano, garlic, bread crumbs, and salt and pepper to taste. Knead the ingredients until well blended. Flour a flat surface and spread the meat mixture on it in an oval shape. Place the hard-boiled eggs lengthwise in the middle of meat mixture. Fold the meat over the eggs and shape into a cylinder. Oil a medium size (9 x 13 x 2½ inch) baking pan with the oilve oil and place the roll in the center. Add 1 cup of water and bake for about 1¼ hours. Remove from the oven and let it cool for 15 minutes before slicing.

Serves 6.

MOUSAKA
(Mousakas)

This is the best dish of the Greek cuisine.

4 large eggplants
1 cup vegetable oil for frying the eggplants
¼ cup olive oil
1 large onion, finely chopped
3 cloves garlic, finely chopped
¼ cup finely chopped fresh parsley
2 tablespoons fresh chopped mint
2 tablespoons finely chopped fresh basil
2½ pounds ground lamb or beef
¼ cup white wine
1 teaspoon ground cinnamon
salt and pepper
1 (16 ounce) can crushed tomatoes
¼ cup dried bread crumbs
½ cup grated kefalotyri cheese
béchamel sauce, see page 68

Preheat oven to 350 degrees F.

❑ Peel and wash the eggplants. Slice them lengthwise into 1 inch slices. Put the eggplants into a large bowl with enough water to cover. Add 1 tablespoon of salt, and let them sit in it for an hour to rid them of bitterness. Remove eggplants and place on paper towels and pat dry. In a large skillet, heat the vegetable oil and fry the eggplants on both sides until light brown. Drain on paper towels and set aside. Heat the olive oil in a medium pot. Add the onion, garlic, parsley, mint and basil. Sauté for 5 minutes. Add the ground meat and sauté until barely brown. Add the wine while continuously stirring to break up any lumps. Add cinnamon, salt and pepper to taste, and crushed tomatoes with juice. Cover the pot and simmer over medium heat for 25 to 30 minutes. Remove from the stove and let cool for 5 minutes. Add bread crumbs and ½ cup kefalotyri cheese to the meat sauce and mix it well. Arrange half of the eggplants on the bottom of a 10 x 15 inch baking pan, sprinkle with ¼ cup of the cheese and cover the eggplants with an even layer of the meat mixture. Layer the remaining eggplants on top of the meat mixture. Spread the béchamel sauce over the eggplants and sprinkle the top with the remaining cheese. Bake for 1 hour or until the top is a golden brown. Remove from the oven and let it cool for 20 minutes before cutting. Delicious.

Serves 8.

STUFFED CABBAGE WITH EGG LEMON SAUCE
(Dolathes Augolemono)

1 large cabbage, 3½ to 4 pounds
2 pounds ground lamb or beef
½ cup rice, uncooked
1 large onion, finely chopped
½ cup fresh parsley, finely chopped
½ cup fresh dill, finely chopped
3 eggs
salt and pepper
¼ cup olive oil
juice of 1 or 2 lemons

❏ Remove the stem of the cabbage. Blanch the cabbage in a large pot of boiling water for 25 to 30 minutes. Set the cabbage aside to drain and cool. When the cabbage is cool enough to handle, remove the leaves, one by one, and set them aside to cool. In a large bowl, mix the meat, rice, onion, parsley, dill, 1 egg, and salt and pepper. Knead the mixture very well. Place 1½ tablespoons of the stuffing near the base of each cabbage leaf, fold in the sides and roll up. Place the stuffed cabbage rolls into a large pot open-side down and sprinkle them with salt and pepper to taste. Pour the olive oil over. Add enough water to cover the rolls in the pot and place a plate on top of the stuffed cabbage. Cover the pot and simmer over medium heat for 1 hour or until there is about 2 cups of sauce remaining. In a blender, beat the 2 eggs and lemon juice for 5 minutes. Slowly add 1 cup of the hot stock to the egg mixture while blending for 2 minutes. Pour the egg mixture over the rolls in the pot , reduce the heat, and simmer 10 minutes. Do not let this boil and do not stir. Serve hot.

Serves 8.

STUFFED CABBAGE WITH TOMATO SAUCE
(Dolmades Me Domata)

1 large cabbage, 3½ to 4 pounds
2½ pounds ground beef or lamb
½ cup rice, uncooked
1 large onion, finely chopped
½ cup fresh parsley, finely chopped
1 teaspoon dried mint
1 teaspoon dried basil
1 egg
½ cup grated kefalotyri cheese
2 cloves garlic, crushed
salt and pepper
28 ounces crushed tomatoes, canned
¼ cup olive oil
2 bay leaves

❏ Remove the stem of the cabbage. Blanch it in a large pot of boiling water for 25 to 30 minutes. Set the cabbage aside to drain and cool. When the cabbage is cool enough to handle, remove leaves one by one and set aside to cool.

❏ In a large bowl, mix the ground meat, rice, onion, parsley, mint, basil, egg, cheese, garlic, and salt and pepper to taste. Knead the mixture well. Place 1½ tablespoons of stuffing at the base of each leaf, fold in the sides and roll up. Place the cabbage rolls, the tomatoes, olive oil, and bay leaves into a large pot; add salt and pepper to taste and enough water to cover the cabbage rolls. Place a plate on top of the stuffed cabbage leaves, cover and simmer over medium-heat for 1 hour and 15 minutes. Most of the water will evaporate. Serve with salad and fresh bread.

Serves 6.

STUFFED
CABBAGE
LEAVES

STUFFED EGGPLANT
(Gemista Papoutsakia)

4 medium eggplants
1 cup vegetable oil, for frying
¼ cup olive oil
1 large onion, chopped
3 cloves garlic, crushed
¼ cup fresh chopped parsley
1 tablespoon fresh chopped basil
2 pounds ground lamb or beef
1 stick cinnamon
1 can (16 ounces) crushed tomatoes
salt and pepper
1 cup grated kefalotyri or romano cheese
¼ cup dried bread crumbs
béchamel sauce, see page 68

Preheat the oven to 350 degrees F.

❑ Wash the eggplant. Cut each one in half horizontally. Scoop out the pulp. Put the eggplant into a large bowl and cover with water and 1 tablespoon salt, soak for 1 hour to rid them of their bitterness. Remove the eggplants and pat dry. Place on paper towels. Place the vegetable oil in a large skillet and heat until hot. Add the eggplants and lightly fry on both sides until softened. Remove and place on a paper towel. In a medium saucepan, heat the olive oil. Add the onion, garlic, parsley, and basil, and sauté for 3 minutes. Add the ground meat and stir until brown. Add cinnamon stick, tomatoes with juice, salt and pepper to taste, and ½ cup water. Cover the saucepan and simmer for 20 to 25 minutes. Remove from the stove and let cool for 15 minutes. Remove cinnamon stick. Add ½ cup of the cheese and the bread crumbs and mix. Place the eggplant in an oiled 9 x 13 x 2½ inch baking pan. Fill each eggplant with the meat mixture. Top each eggplant with béchamel sauce and sprinkle with cheese. Bake for 40 to 45 minutes or until sauce turns golden brown. Serve hot.

Serves 8.

STUFFED TOMATOES
(Domates Yemistes)

8 to 10 large tomatoes
salt and pepper
¼ cup olive oil
2 pounds ground lean beef
1 large onion, finely chopped
3 cloves garlic, chopped
3 tablespoons fresh parsley, finely chopped
2 tablespoons fresh mint, chopped
2 tablespoons fresh basil, finely chopped
1 can (8 ounces) crushed tomatoes
¼ cup white wine
½ cup rice, uncooked
½ cup grated kefalotyri or romano cheese, plus
   additional for topping

Preheat the oven to 350 degrees F.

❑ Square off the bottom of each tomato so it will stand up. Slice off the top and carefully clean out the inside of each tomato, removing the pulp and seeds. Save the tops and sprinkle some salt and pepper on the tomatoes and set aside. Heat the olive oil in a large pan and add the ground meat, onions, garlic, parsley, mint, basil, and crushed tomatoes, wine, rice, salt and pepper to taste, and 1 cup of water. Cover the pan and let it simmer on low heat for about 20 minutes, or until the juice is absorbed. Take the pan off the stove and add the cheese. Mix well.

❑ Using a teaspoon, fill the tomatoes with the stuffing, and place in a greased baking pan. Cover each tomato with the top piece that was cut off and drizzle them with 2 tablespoons olive oil and a little tomato juice. Sprinkle additional cheese on the tomatoes. Bake for 45 minutes to 1 hour.

Serves 6.

STUFFED ZUCCHINI
(Kolokithakia Yemista)

6 zucchini
½ cup olive oil
1 large onion, chopped
2 cloves garlic, crushed
2 tablespoons finely chopped fresh parsley
2 tablespoons finely chopped basil
1½ pounds ground lamb or beef
½ cup rice, uncooked
1 cup (16 ounces) crushed tomatoes
salt and pepper
½ cup grated kefalotyri cheese plus additional for
   topping

Preheat the oven to 350 degrees F.

❏ Trim and wash the zucchini. Cut each one in half lengthwise. Using a teaspoon, carefully remove the pulp. Heat ¼
cup oil in a large pan and add the onion, garlic, parsley
and basil. Sauté until tender. Add the meat and brown it,
stirring for 10 minutes. Add the rice and stir well. Add the
crushed tomatoes, 1 cup of water, and salt and pepper to
taste. Cover the pot and let it simmer on medium heat for
15 to 20 minutes. Take it off the stove, add kefalotyri
cheese and mix. Cool. Fill the zucchini shells with the meat
mixture and arrange them in a baking pan. Add 1 cup of
water and ¼ cup oil to the bottom of the pan. Sprinkle with
kefalotyri cheese, cover and bake for about 1 hour.

Serve with a salad.

Serves 6.

AROMATIC ROAST LEG OF LAMB
(Arni Aromatiko)

The mouth-watering aroma of the meat spices gives the lamb a delicious flavor.

6 to 7 pound leg of lamb (bone in or out)
1 stick of cinnamon
8 peppercorns
3 whole cloves
4 cloves garlic, crushed
2 tablespoons chopped fresh mint
4 to 5 leaves fresh sage
3 tablespoons olive oil
3 tablespoons lemon juice
1 tablespoon dried oregano
salt
½ cup white wine
parsley for garnish
lemon slices for garnish

Preheat the oven to 350 degrees F.

❑ Trim the excess fat from the lamb. Wash it and pat dry. Place the lamb in a large roasting pan and set aside. In a blender, food processor, or with mortar and pestle, grind the cinnamon stick, peppercorns, whole cloves, garlic, mint and sage together. Add the oil, lemon juice, oregano and salt to taste. Blend all together. With a sharp knife, cut 6 to 7 slits into the lamb and insert the spice mixture deep into the slits; spread the remaining mixture on top of the lamb, covering the whole meat surface. Add 2 to 3 cups of water to the bottom of the pan. (Do not pour water over the meat.) When the lamb has cooked for 1 hour, pour the wine on top of the meat. Bake for 2 hours. Baste from time to time. Remove from the oven, let stand for 5 minutes. Cut the lamb and arrange slices on a large platter. Pour the remaining juices over the lamb and garnish with parsley and slices of lemon. Serve with rice and salad (optional).

Serves 8.

BAKED LAMB WITH POTATOES
(Arni Me Patates Sto Fourno)

1 leg of lamb, 6 to 7 pounds (bone in or out)
2 lemons
salt and pepper
2 teaspoons dried oregano
5 whole cloves garlic
1 tablespoon crushed garlic
¼ cup olive oil
8 large potatoes

Preheat the oven to 350 degrees F.

❑ Wash and trim all the excess fat off the lamb. Drain. Squeeze the juice of 1 lemon over the leg of lamb. Add salt and pepper to taste and sprinkle with 1 teaspoon oregano. With a sharp knife, make some small slits in the side of the leg. Insert whole cloves of garlic into the holes and rub the leg with half of the crushed garlic. Place the leg of lamb in a large baking pan. Drizzle the lamb with the olive oil and add 1 cup of water to the pan. Bake for 45 minutes. Peel the potatoes; wash and cut them into quarters. Place the potatoes into a large bowl and sprinkle them with the juice of 1 lemon, and salt and pepper to taste, 1 teaspoon oregano and the remaining crushed garlic.

❑ Remove lamb from the oven and place the potatoes around the leg of lamb in the baking pan. Add 2 cups of water and bake together for 1½ hours. Baste the lamb with its own juices as it cooks. Remove the lamb from the oven and let it stand for 5 minutes. Slice and arrange on a large platter. Add the potatoes around the lamb; garnish with lemon slices.

Serves 8.

LAMB and POTATOES

LAMB FRICASSEE
(Arni Fricase)

3½ to 4 pounds shoulder of lamb or combination
¼ cup olive oil
1 cup chopped scallions
1 large oninon, chopped
salt and pepper
1 large head romaine lettuce
¼ cup fresh chopped dill
¼ cup fresh chopped parsley
2 eggs
juice of 1 lemon

❑ Wash and drain the meat. Put into a medium pot with the olive oil and brown lightly. Add the scallions and onion and stir 2 to 3 minutes. Add 3 cups of water and salt and pepper to taste, and bring to a slow boil. Let it simmer for about 1 hour. Wash the lettuce and discard the outer leaves. Cut each of the lettuce leaves into 3 to 4 pieces and toss in a large bowl with the dill and parsley. Add to the meat with 2 cups water. Bring to a boil and simmer for 45 minutes, until the lamb and lettuce are cooked.

❑ Beat the eggs, add the lemon juice and blend thoroughly. Add 1 cup of stock from the pot slowly to the eggs, while continuing to blend. Beat for 2-3 minutes. Slowly add this mixture to the pot of meat stirring thoroughly. Remove the pot from the stove and serve hot.

Serves 6.

LAMB WITH GREEN BEANS AND TOMATO SAUCE
(Arni Me Fasolakia Kokinisto)

3½ to 4 pounds lamb, leg, shoulder or combination
¼ cup olive oil
1 large onion, chopped
2 cloves garlic, finely chopped
salt and pepper
1 can (16 ounces) crushed tomatoes
1½ pounds green beans
¼ cup fresh chopped parsley
2 bay leaves

❏ Trim any excess fat off the meat; wash and drain. Heat the oil in a medium saucepan. Add the meat and sauté until barely brown. Add the onion and garlic and sauté for 2 minutes or until tender. Add salt and pepper to taste. Add the tomatoes and 3 cups of water. Cover and simmer on medium heat for 1 hour.

❏ Wash and clean the green beans. Cut them in half and add to the lamb together with the parsley, bay leaves and 1 cup of water. Lower the heat and cover the pot. Let it simmer for 45 minutes or more. If more water is needed, add a little, but this sauce should not be thin.

Serve with bread and feta cheese.

Serves 6.

GRILLED LAMB CHOPS
(Brizoles Sti Sxara)

4 to 5 lamb chops, 1½ pounds
¼ cup olive oil
1 teaspoon dried oregano
¼ cup white wine
juice of 1 lemon
1 teaspoon crushed garlic
salt and pepper
2 bay leaves

❑ Wash the chops and remove the excess fat. Beat them with a meat tenderizer on a wood cutting board. In a large bowl, mix the oil, oregano, wine, lemon juice, garlic, and salt and pepper to taste. Beat until blended; add bay leaves and marinate the lamb chops in the mixture for 1 hour in the refrigerator. Preheat the grill and sear in the meat juices at a medium temperature, about 30 minutes total. Throw away excess marinade and do not use on cooked meat.

Serve with a Greek salad.

Serves 4.

LAMB KAPAMA
(Arni Kapamas)

¼ cup olive oil
1 large onion, chopped
2 cloves garlic, crushed
3½ to 4 pounds lamb, boneless or combination
¼ cup white wine
salt and pepper
1 can (16 ounces) tomato sauce
2 sticks cinnamon
3 whole cloves
1 sprig fresh rosemary
2 bay leaves

❏ In a medium saucepan, heat the oil, add the onion and garlic, and sauté for 2 minutes. Add the meat and lightly brown. Add the wine and stir. Add the tomato sauce, cinnamon, cloves, rosemary, bay leaves and 3 cups of water. Cover and let simmer for 1½ hour over medium heat or until the sauce is thick. Add water if necessary. Serve hot with any pasta or rice.

Serves 6.

LAMB KEBOBS
(Souvlaki)

3½ to 4 pounds of boneless lamb
salt and pepper
2 large onions
3 medium green peppers
3 large ripe tomatoes or cherry tomatoes
½ cup olive oil
½ cup white wine
¼ cup lemon juice
1 teaspoon dried oregano
3 cloves garlic, crushed
3 bay leaves
1 teaspoon dried basil
 tzatziki sauce, see page 69

❑ Wash and drain the meat. Cut into 2-inch cubes and put into a large bowl. Sprinkle with salt and pepper to taste. Peel the onions and quarter and separate into pieces. Clean the peppers and quarter them also. Add the onions and peppers to the meat. Mix together oil, wine, the lemon juice, oregano, garlic, bay leaves and basil. Mix well. Pour over meat and vegetables. Cover the bowl, refrigerate meat in marinade overnight. On wood or metal skewers, arrange pieces of pepper, onion, meat and tomato. Place them in a broiler pan. Broil for 15 minutes on each side.

Serve hot with rice pilaf and tzatziki sauce.

Serves 8.

LAMB WITH OKRA

This dish not only tastes great but looks very tempting.

4 to 4½ pounds lamb; leg, shoulder or combination
¼ cup olive oil
1 onion, chopped
2 cloves garlic, chopped
¼ cup white wine
1 can (16 ounces) crushed tomatoes
1½ pounds fresh or frozen okra
¼ cup white vinegar
¼ cup fresh chopped parsley
1 tablespoon fresh chopped basil
salt and pepper

❑ Cut the lamb into serving pieces. Wash and pat dry. Heat the oil in a large saucepan and sauté the onions, garlic and meat. Add the wine, tomatoes with their juice and 3 cups of water. Cover and simmer on medium heat for 1½ hours.

❑ Prepare the okra by cutting off the tops. Place the okra on a large platter and sprinkle with vinegar. Let stand for 30 minutes. Remove only the lamb pieces from the saucepan. Keep covered throughout the process. Add the okra to the remaining sauce and 1½ to 2 cups of water. Add the parsley, basil and salt and pepper to taste and cover. Cook for 20 to 30 minutes, or until the okra is almost tender. Add the meat that was put aside, and continue cooking 10 minutes.

❑ Arrange the meat on a large platter, and surround it with the okra.

Serves 6.

BAKED LAMB WITH SPAGHETTI
(Arni Me Makaronia)

4 to 4½ pounds boneless lamb (or combination
  with bone in)
¼ cup olive oil
4 cloves garlic, crushed
¼ cup white wine
1 can (28 ounces) crushed tomatoes
salt and pepper
1 pound spaghetti
1 cup grated kefalotyri or romano cheese

Preheat the oven to 350 degrees F.

❏ Trim off excess fat; wash and pat the meat dry. Heat the oil
in a large saucepan and sauté the meat and garlic for 10
minutes. Add the wine and stir. Add the tomatoes with
juice, salt and pepper. Add 3 cups of water. Cover and cook
on medium heat for 20 minutes. Remove from the heat and
place the meat with sauce into a baking pan. Add 4 cups
water and bake for 1 hour. Remove lamb and put it aside
on a platter. Return sauce to the oven and allow the juices
to boil. Break the spaghetti in half and add to the sauce.
Make sure the liquid covers the spaghetti. Stir and let it
bake in the oven about 30 minutes. Return the lamb pieces
to the pan and bake an additional 10 minutes or until the
spaghetti is thoroughly cooked. Remove the pan from the
oven and let cool 5 minutes. Arrange the lamb on a platter.
Remove the spaghetti. Put it on a separate dish and sprinkle with the cheese. Serve hot.

Serves 8.

EGGPLANT STUFFED WITH GROUND LAMB
(Melitzanes Yemistes)

10 to 12 small Italian eggplants for stuffing
¼ cup olive oil
1 large onion, chopped
2 cloves garlic, crushed
¼ cup fresh parsley, finely chopped
2 teaspoons chopped fresh basil
2 tablespoons fresh mint, finely chopped
1½ pounds ground lamb or beef
¼ cup rice
salt and pepper
8 ounce can tomato sauce
½ cup grated kefalotyri cheese, plus additional for
   topping

Preheat the oven to 350 degrees F.

❑ Clean the eggplants and cut off the tops. Carefully scoop out most of the insides. Half fill a large pot with water. Add a little salt and bring it to a boil. Add the eggplants and boil for about 5 minutes, or until tender. Pour into a colander to drain.

❑ Heat the oil in a medium pot and add the onion, garlic, parsley, basil and mint. Sauté until tender. Add the ground meat and cook until slightly browned. Add rice, salt and pepper to taste, tomato sauce, 1 cup of water and stir.

❑ Cover the pan and let it simmer for another 10 to 15 minutes. Take it off the stove and let it cool for 5 minutes. Add ½ cup cheese to the mixture.

❏ With a teaspoon fill each eggplant with the stuffing. Arrange the stuffed eggplants in a medium-size (9 x 13 x 2½ inch) oiled baking pan approximately 1 inch apart. Dribble some oil on top of the eggplants and add 1 cup of water to the bottom of the pan. Sprinkle some cheese on top. Bake for 1 hour.

Serves 6.

STUFFED ROAST LAMB WITH FETA CHEESE
(Arni Gemisto Me Feta)

1 leg of lamb, 6 to 7 pounds, boneless
1 tablespoon dried oregano
1 tablespoon dried thyme
salt and pepper
¼ cup fresh parsley, chopped
4 cloves garlic, crushed
1½ cup crumbled feta cheese
½ cup olive oil
juice of 2 lemons
½ cup white wine
lemon slices for garnish
parsley for garnish

Preheat the oven to 350 degrees F.

❏ Trim the excess fat from the lamb. Wash and pat dry. Open the leg of lamb so that it lies flat. Pound lightly to make a flat surface for stuffing. Sprinkle half of the oregano, half the thyme, and salt and pepper to taste in a small bowl. Add the parsley, garlic, feta cheese and 2 tablespoons olive oil plus 3 tablespoons of lemon juice, and mix. Place this mixture at the short end of the piece of lamb and roll up. Tie with a string 5 to 6 times to secure. Place it all into a large baking pan. Squeeze the juice of 1 lemon over it, and sprinkle with remaining garlic, oregano, thyme, salt and pepper and oil. Add 1 cup of water and the wine to the bottom of the pan. Bake for 2 hours.

❑ Add water to the pan when necessary and baste with the juices from time to time. Take out of the oven and let it cool for 5 minutes. Place the lamb on a large platter and slice the meat. Garnish with lemon slices and parsley.

Serve with rice or baked potatoes.

Serves 8.

FRIED LIVER
(Sikotia Tiganita)

1½ to 2 pounds liver, beef or lamb
salt and pepper
juice of 1 lemon
1 tablespoon dry oregano
2 cloves garlic, crushed
1 cup bread crumbs
1 cup flour
2 eggs
2 cups milk
1 cup vegetable oil

❑ Cut the liver into long wide strips. Put in a large bowl and add salt and pepper to taste. Sprinkle with the lemon juice, oregano, and garlic. Let stand 10 minutes. Put the bread crumbs on one plate and flour on another. In a medium bowl, beat eggs for 2 to 3 minutes. Take each strip of liver and flour lightly. Dip it in the egg mixture and cover with bread crumbs. Put oil into a large skillet and heat until very hot. Fry 5 to 6 strips of the liver at a time on both sides for 15 to 20 minutes until golden brown. Drain on paper towels and serve hot.

Serves 4.

PORK WITH CELERY AND EGG LEMON SAUCE
(Xirino Me Celino Augolemono)

4¼ pounds lean pork shoulder or country style ribs
¼ cup olive oil
1 large onion, chopped
¼ cup fresh chopped parsley
1 large bunch celery stalks, cut into 4- to 5-inch
    pieces
2 large carrots, sliced
2 eggs
juice of 1 lemon

❑ Wash and pat dry the meat. In a large saucepan, heat the oil. Add onion and parsley and sauté for 3 minutes. Add the meat and lightly brown on both sides. Add 3 cups of water and cover. Simmer for 1 hour. Add celery, carrots, 1 cup of water and cover. Reduce the heat to medium and simmer 35 to 40 minutes. Add 2 cups of liquid to the drippings that are left in the pan. In a blender, beat the eggs for 5 minutes and add lemon juice. While beating continuously, slowly add 1 cup of the hot stock from the saucepan to the egg mixture. Stir the egg mixture back into the saucepan, slowly, over low heat for 1 to 2 minutes. Do not let it boil. This delicious dish should be served hot.

Serves 6.

PORK WITH WINE SAUCE
(Hirino Ladorigano)

This is a very tasty dish. Serve with mashed potatoes and a salad.

    3½ to 4 pounds pork shoulder or chops
    juice of 1 lemon
    ¼ cup olive oil
    ½ cup white wine
    3 cloves garlic, crushed
    1 teaspoon dried oregano
    2 bay leaves
    salt and pepper

❏ Wash and trim the excess fat from the meat. Put into a large bowl and sprinkle with the lemon juice. Heat the oil in large pot and brown the meat. Add the wine, garlic, oregano, bay leaves, and salt and pepper to taste and sauté for 5 minutes. Add 1 cup of water. Cover the pot and let it simmer on medium heat for 1 hour, or until the meat is tender. Add ½ cup of water during the cooking process as necessary. Serve hot.

Serves 6.

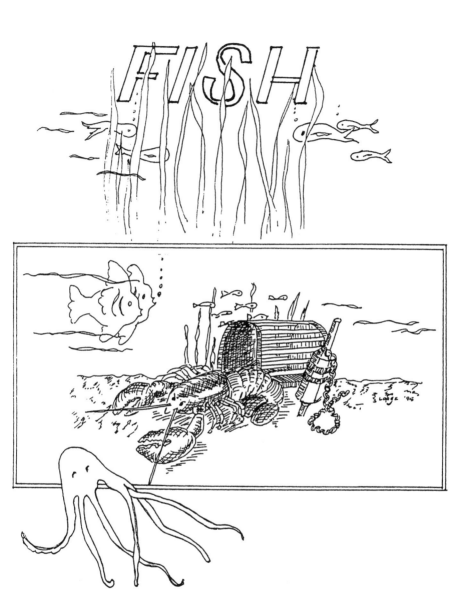

FISH SOUP
(Psarosoupa)

2 pounds fish filet (haddock, cod or red snapper)
3 potatoes, cut into quarters
2 carrots, sliced
3 stalks celery, cut into 2 inch pieces
4 small whole white onions
1 pint cherry tomatoes
¼ cup olive oil
½ cup rice
salt and pepper

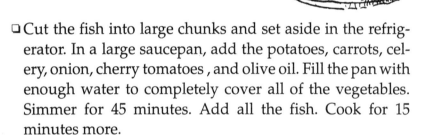

❑ Cut the fish into large chunks and set aside in the refrigerator. In a large saucepan, add the potatoes, carrots, celery, onion, cherry tomatoes , and olive oil. Fill the pan with enough water to completely cover all of the vegetables. Simmer for 45 minutes. Add all the fish. Cook for 15 minutes more.

❑ Gently remove the fish first and place on a large platter. Then remove the remaining vegetables and surround the fish with them. Strain the remaining sauce and return it to the pan. Add 2 or 3 cups of water and bring it to a boil. Add the rice and salt and pepper and cover. Stir occasionally to keep the rice from sticking to the pan. Cook until the rice is done, making sure the soup doesn't get too thick, about 20 minutes. Season with salt and pepper to taste. Serve the soup hot and complement it with a side dish of the warmed fish and vegetables.

Serves 6.

FISH SOUP WITH EGG AND LEMON SAUCE
(Psarosoupa Ayogolemono)

2 pounds haddock
3 potatoes, cut into quarters
2 carrots, sliced
3 sticks celery, chopped (1 inch pieces)
6 small whole onions
¼ cup olive oil
salt and pepper
½ cup rice
2 eggs
juice of 2 lemons

❑ Wash the fish and pat it dry. Cut it into chunks and set aside in the refrigerator. In a large saucepan, add all of the vegetables, oil, salt and pepper and cover completely with 3 quarts of water. Bring to a boil for 40 minutes. Add the fish and cook for 15 minutes. Remove the saucepan from the heat, and with a slotted spoon arrange the fish and vegetables on a large platter. Strain the remaining stock into a clean saucepan. Add 1 cup of water and return to a boil. Add the rice, cover and boil for 20 minutes.

❑ In the blender, beat the eggs and lemon juice for 5 minutes. While continuing to process, add 1 cup of the hot fish stock to the egg mixture. Reduce the heat to very low and add the egg mixture to the saucepan. Stir constantly for 2 minutes. Serve hot with the platter of the warmed vegetables and fish. Delicious.

Serves 6.

FRIED FISH
(Tiganito Yari)

1½ to 2 pounds haddock or cod
salt
juice of 2 lemons, divided
1 cup flour
½ cup corn flour
2 eggs
2 cups milk
1 cup vegetable oil
lemon slices for garnish
parsley for garnish

❑ Wash and pat dry the fish. Cut into 6 ounce serving pieces. Put on a large platter and sprinkle with salt to taste and juice of 1 lemon. Let stand in the refrigerator for 30 minutes. Mix flour and corn flour. In a medium bowl beat eggs and milk for 5 minutes. Dip the fish in the egg mixture. Flour each piece, removing excess flour. In a large skillet, heat oil until very hot. Add 2 to 3 pieces of fish and fry 5 to 6 minutes each on both sides until golden brown. Place fish on a large platter, top with lemon slices and garnish with parsley.

Serve hot.

Serves 5 to 6.

Corn flour (finely ground corn meal) can be purchased at many supermarkets or a Mediterranean store.

FRIED MUSSELS
(Mithia Tiganta)

2½ to 3 pounds fresh mussels
1 lemon
salt and pepper
2 eggs
1½ cups milk
1 cup flour
1 cup corn flour
1½ cups vegetable oil (for frying)

❏ Wash and clean the mussels thoroughly, making sure to get rid of all the sand. Put the mussels into a pot and cover them with water. Boil for 5 to 6 minutes or until they open. Remove the pot from the stove and drain. Open the mussels and remove meat. Put the meat into a colander and rinse with cold water. Drain. Sprinkle with the juice of 1 lemon, and salt and pepper.

❏ In a medium bowl, beat the eggs and milk. On a large platter, mix the flour with the corn flour. Heat the oil in a frying pan until it is very hot. Dip the mussels in the egg mixture and then into the flour and fry them to a golden brown.

❏ Serve with lemon, fresh bread and ouzo or a good wine.

Serves 6.

Corn flour can be purchased at many supermarkets or a Mediterranean store.

FRIED SWORDFISH Plaki
(Tiganito Swordfish Plaki)

2 pounds swordfish
juice of 1 lemon
1 cup flour
1 cup oil (for frying)
¼ cup olive oil
1 cup chopped onion
3 cloves garlic, crushed
1 tablespoon fresh chopped basil, plus additional
    for topping
1 tablespoon fresh chopped parsley, plus additional
    for topping
¼ cup white wine
salt and pepper
1 can (16 ounces) crushed tomatoes

❑ Wash the fish and pat it dry. Cut into serving-size pieces. Sprinkle with lemon juice and let stand for 20 minutes. Lightly flour each piece of fish. In hot oil fry the fish on both sides until golden brown. Place the fish on a large platter and keep warm.

❑ In a medium saucepan, heat the olive oil and add the onion, garlic, basil and parsley. Stir together until limp, about 5 minutes. Add the wine, salt and pepper to taste, tomatoes with juice and ½ cup of water. Cover the pan and let it simmer for 20 to 25 minutes until the sauce thickens. Remove from the heat. Spoon the hot sauce over the warm fish and sprinkle with parsley and basil.

Serves 4.

GREEK CAVIAR
(Taramosalata)

A tasty dip served with crackers.

1 loaf firm bread (1 pound)
½ cup tarama (carp roe caviar)
1 cup olive oil
½ cup lemon juice
½ cup chopped scallions
pepper
¼ cup fresh finely chopped parsley

❏ Cut the crust off the bread and soak the bread in water, then squeeze out excess and set bread aside. Place the tarama in a blender, and add the oil a little at a time. Keep beating the tarama and add the soaked bread slowly until the two are mixed well. Add lemon juice and more oil if necessary for a paste-like consistency. Mix in the scallions and season with pepper. Serve on a medium-deep platter and sprinkle the parsley on top.

Yields 3 cups.

ISLAND-STYLE SHRIMP
(Nisiotikes Garides)

1 pound shrimp, cooked
¼ cup olive oil
¼ cup white wine
2 cloves garlic, crushed
½ teaspoon dried mint
½ teaspoon dried oregano
1 teaspoon dried basil
1 teaspoon pepper flakes
salt and pepper

❑ Rinse the shrimp, remove their shells and devein. Heat the oil in a large skillet and add the shrimp. Stir for 2 minutes and add the wine, garlic, mint, oregano, basil, pepper flakes, and salt and pepper to taste. Stir constantly for 15 minutes. Serve hot. Makes a great appetizer.

Serves 4.

LOBSTER DELIGHT WITH PASTA
(Astako Megalio)

2 lobsters, 1½ to 2 pounds each
¼ cup olive oil
1 large onion, chopped
2 tablespoons fresh parsley, chopped
2 cloves garlic, crushed
2 tablespoons fresh chopped basil
¼ cup white wine
1 can (16 ounces) stewed tomatoes
2 bay leaves
salt and pepper
1 pound of your favorite pasta
1 cup grated kefalotyri cheese

❑ Fill a lobster pot half full of water. Bring it to a full boil, drop in the lobsters and boil for 15 minutes. Remove them and put aside to cool. Reserve the stock. When the lobsters are cool enough to handle, crack the shells and remove the meat. Cut the meat into large chunks and put aside. Heat the oil in a medium saucepan and add the onions, parsley, garlic and basil. Sauté until tender. Add the wine and stir all ingredients. Add the tomatoes, bay leaves and 2 cups of lobster stock. Add salt and pepper to taste. Cover the pan and lower the heat to medium and simmer for 20 to 25 minutes. Add the lobster to the saucepan. Simmer for an additional 10 to 15 minutes.

❑ Prepare the pasta according to package instructions, drain and arrange on a large serving platter. Sprinkle with ½ cup of the kefalotyri cheese and pour the lobster sauce over the pasta. Sprinkle with remaining ½ cup of cheese.

Serve hot with any salad of your choice.

Serves 6.

OCTOPUS IN TOMATO SAUCE
(Htapothi Me Tomata)

3 pounds fresh octopus
¼ cup olive oil
1 large onion, chopped
4 or 5 cloves garlic, finely chopped
¼ cup red wine
2 sticks cinnamon
3 whole cloves
2 bay leaves
1 (8 ounce) can tomato sauce
salt and pepper

❏ Clean the octopus very well and cut it into 4 inch pieces. In a medium saucepan, heat the oil and add the octopus. Add the onion and garlic and sauté for 5 minutes. Slowly add the wine together with the spices. Add tomato sauce, 1 cup water, and salt and pepper to taste. Cover the pot and simmer for 45 minutes to 1 hour until the sauce is considerably reduced. Add additional water if necessary.

Serves 6.

SAUTÉED OCTOPUS WITH OLIVES
(Htapodi Me Ellies)

3 pounds octopus
¼ cup olive oil
2 cloves garlic, crushed
1 large onion, chopped
¼ cup red wine
3 whole cloves
salt and pepper
1 cup pitted green olives

❑ Cut the octopus into 4-inch pieces. Wash and drain. In a medium saucepan, put the octopus and 1 cup of water. Simmer until all the water is absorbed (10 to 15 minutes). Add the oil, garlic, onion and sauté for 5 minutes. Add the wine, cloves, salt and pepper to taste, and 1 cup of water. Cover and simmer on low heat for 45 minutes to 1 hour. Most of the water will be absorbed. Add the olives and cook an additional 15 minutes.

❑ Remove from the heat and let cool for 5 minutes. Place the octopus on a large platter and serve as an appetizer.

Serves 4.

SHRIMP WITH LINGUINI
(Garides Apo Ta Psara)

1 to 1½ pounds shrimp, cooked
¼ cup olive oil
1 large onion, chopped
1 large green pepper, chopped
½ cup celery, chopped
2 cloves garlic, crushed
¼ cup fresh parsley, chopped
¼ cup red wine
4 large ripe blanched and crushed tomatoes
2 bay leaves
salt and pepper
1 pound linguini pasta
¾ cup grated romano cheese

❑ Thoroughly rinse the shrimp. Remove the shells and devein. Set aside in a colander and let drain. Heat the oil in a saucepan and add the onions, green peppers, celery, garlic and parsley. Sauté until tender. Add the wine, tomatoes, bay leaves, 1 cup of water, and salt and pepper to taste. Simmer over medium heat for 35 to 40 minutes. Add the shrimp and stir all together. Cover the pot and simmer for 15 minutes or until the sauce thickens and all the flavors mix well with the shrimp.

❑ Prepare the pasta according to package directions and place it on a large platter. Top with the shrimp and the sauce, and sprinkle with the cheese. Serve hot.

Serves 6.

SQUID WITH SPINACH
(Kalamarakia Mr Spanaki)

1½ pounds squid, cleaned
¼ cup olive oil
2 large onions, chopped
2 cloves garlic, crushed
1 can (16 ounces) crushed tomatoes
2 packages (10 ounces each) fresh spinach
¼ cup fresh dill, finely chopped
salt and pepper

❏ Wash the squid and separate the body from the tentacles. Cut each body into 2-inch rings. Chop the tentacles into small pieces. Place squid in a colander and thoroughly drain. Heat the oil in a pot and add the onion, garlic and squid. Sauté until the onion is tender, about 5 minutes. Add the tomatoes with juice and simmer for about 20 minutes.

❏ Cut the spinach into pieces. Wash and drain. Add the spinach and dill to the pot with the squid and sprinkle some salt and pepper on top. Cover and simmer for 20 to 25 minutes over a low heat. It is done when most of the water has evaporated and the oil remains.

Serves 6.

BLACK WALNUT
CAKE

HOLIDAY BREAD

Pastries

WEDDING
COOKIES

WITH
ALMONDS

BAKLAVA

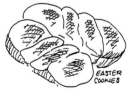

EASTER
COOKIES

THINGS YOU SHOULD KNOW ABOUT PASTRIES

❑ Most of the Greek pastries call for a syrup topping. There are 2 ways to add syrup to a Greek cake: for a hot cake add cold syrup; and, for a cold cake add hot syrup.

❑ Lemon juice, when added to the hot syrup, prevents the syrup from thickening.

❑ When beating egg whites, add two drops of lemon juice to stiffen the egg whites.

❑ When preparing any pastry from fillo dough, after you have brushed the top with butter, sprinkle with a few drops of water. This will hold the shape of the fillo dough and keep it from cracking apart.

❑ When preparing any pastry, make sure you have all of the ingredients pre-measured and ready in front of you, especially the melted butter.

❑ Pastries that need no refrigeration are: baklava, kataifi, kourambiethes, finikia and all cookies.

❑ A flour tip: when a recipe calls for 4 to 5, or 5 to 6 cups, use your own judgment to get the right consistency.

BAKLAVA
(Baklavas)

This is the most popular pastry from Greece.

5 cups coarsely chopped walnuts
½ cup sugar
¼ cup plain dried bread crumbs
1 tablespoon ground cinnamon
1 tablespoon ground cloves
1 cup unsalted butter, melted
1 teaspoon vanilla
1 pound fillo dough

Preheat the oven to 325 degrees F.

❑ In a large bowl, mix the walnuts, sugar, bread crumbs, cinnamon and cloves. Add ¼ cup of the melted butter and the vanilla. Mix together carefully.

❑ Brush butter on all the sides and bottom of a 18 x 12 x 3 inch jelly roll pan . Layer 5 sheets of fillo dough in the pan, brushing each layer with butter. Evenly spread 1½ cups of the walnut mixture over the top layer. Fold in the long sides of the fillo, and brush them with melted butter. Add 3 more fillo sheets, brushing each one with butter. Spread with 1½ cups of walnut mixture, turn the long sides in toward the center and brush with butter. Add 3 more fillo sheets, brushing with butter, and top with remaining walnut mixture. Turn the sides in and continue adding remaining fillo sheets, brushing each with butter. With a sharp knife, cut diagonally across the top to mark into diamond shaped pieces. Brush the top with butter very thoroughly until all sides and top are completely covered.

Sprinkle with water and bake for 1 hour, or until golden brown.

Syrup:
   3 cups sugar
   4 cups water
   ½ cup honey
   1 stick cinnamon
   3 whole cloves
   2 tablespoons lemon juice
   1 slice lemon peel

❑ Mix together all ingredients and boil for 15 minutes. Remove the cinnamon, cloves and lemon peel. Cool completely. Spoon the cold syrup over the hot baklava.

❑ Let the baklava stand at room temperature for 6 hours before serving. Do not refrigerate.

Serves 3 dozen.

BUTTER COOKIES
(Kourambiethes)

These cookies are so delicious that my mother served them at my wedding.

1½ pounds unsalted butter, 6 sticks
4½ cups confectioner's sugar
2 egg yolks
¼ cup ouzo liquor
1 teaspoon vanilla
4 to 5 cups flour
1 teaspoon baking powder
1 cup chopped almonds, roasted

Preheat the oven to 350 degrees F.

❏ Beat the butter and ½ cup of confectioners' sugar until creamy smooth, about 15 minutes. Add the egg yolks, ouzo and vanilla and beat 5 more minutes. In a separate bowl, mix the flour, baking powder and almonds. Add the flour slowly to the butter mixture until it is stiff enough to pinch off a piece and form a ball. Shape tablespoons of the dough into half moons and place on a greased cookie sheet one inch apart. Bake for 20 to 25 minutes then check the bottoms. They will be a golden brown in color when done. The tops, however, should be white. Allow to cool for 5 minutes. Sift confectioners' sugar over warm cookies so that they are heavily coated. Let cool.

Makes 4 to 5 dozen cookies.

CARROT CAKE
(Karroto Keik)

6 eggs
1½ cups sugar
1 cup unsalted butter, melted
¼ cup fresh orange juice
1 teaspoon vanilla
3 cups flour
1 tablespoon baking powder
1 cup grated carrots
¾ cup golden raisins
1 cup coarsely chopped walnuts

Preheat the oven to 350 degrees F.

❑ In a large bowl, cream the eggs with the sugar for 10 minutes. Add the butter, orange juice and vanilla to the mixture. Beat for 5 minutes more. Add the flour, baking powder, carrots, raisins and walnuts and beat for 2 to 3 minutes. Grease and lightly flour a tube pan (bundt). Distribute the cake mixture evenly around the tube. Bake for 1 hour and allow the cake to cool. Serve.

Serves 8.

COFFEE COOKIE TWISTS
(Koulourakia)

These are delicious with coffee or tea for an afternoon treat.

Anise flavoring may be purchased at most supermarkets in the baking ingredients and spice section.

1 cup unsalted butter
½ cup vegetable oil
1½ cups sugar
4 large eggs
¼ cup fresh orange juice
1½ tablespoons anise flavoring
1 teaspoon vanilla
5 to 6 cups flour
4 teaspoons baking powder
½ cup sesame seeds

Preheat the oven to 350 degrees F.

❑ In a large bowl, combine the butter, oil and sugar. Beat until creamy smooth. Add the eggs, orange juice, anise, and vanilla and beat for 10 minutes. Add the flour and baking powder to the batter. With your hands, mold the batter into a firm but soft ball. Let stand for 15 minutes.

❑ Pinch off a piece of dough, about 1½ tablespoons, and roll into a 5-inch rope. Fold rope in half and twist together. Place on a greased cookie sheet, 1 inch apart, then brush with egg wash. Sprinkle sesame seeds on the cookies. Bake for 25 to 30 minutes or until golden brown.

Makes 4 dozen cookies.

CORINTHIAN CAKE
(Korinthos Keik)

5 eggs
1½ cups sugar
½ cup plain yogurt
1 cup unsalted butter, melted
1 teaspoon vanilla
2½ cups flour
2 teaspoons baking powder
1 teaspoon ground cinnamon
1 teaspoon ground cloves
1 tablespoon grated lemon peel
1 cup golden raisins
Preheat the oven to 350 degrees F.

❑ In a large bowl, beat the eggs and sugar until creamy smooth. Add the yogurt, butter and vanilla and beat for 5 minutes. Add the flour, baking powder, cinnamon, cloves, lemon and raisins and mix for 5 minutes more.

❑ Grease and lightly flour a tube pan (bundt) and pour the batter evenly into the pan. Bake for 45 minutes to 1 hour. Allow to cool. Serve with a cup of tea or coffee.

Serves 8.

CUSTARD PIE
(Galaktoboureko)

5 cups milk
¾ cup farina semolina
5 eggs
1 cup sugar
1 tablespoon grated lemon peel
1 teaspoon vanilla
1 cup unsalted butter, melted
1 pound fillo dough

Preheat the oven to 350 degrees F.

❑ Heat the milk in a medium-size saucepan and add the farina slowly. Stir constantly until thickened. Remove from the heat and pour into a separate bowl. Mix the eggs, sugar, lemon and vanilla, plus ¼ cup of the butter. Beat for 5 minutes. Then, with a ladle, slowly add about 1 cup of the farina mixture to the egg mixture. Mix gently but thoroughly; then add the egg mixture to the farina mixture, making sure to continue stirring. Return to low heat to cook for 5 minutes for a nice smooth texture. Remove from the stove.

❑ Grease a 9 x 13 x 2½ inch pan and line the bottom with 10 buttered fillo dough leaves, crisscrossing them with 5 in one direction and 5 in the other. Pour the cream over them. Place the rest of the fillo leaves on top of the cream, brushing each one with butter and trimming off any excess. Brush the top leaf with butter then sprinkle with water. Mark the top leaves diagonally with a sharp knife into serving-size diamond shapes. Do not cut through the entire pastry. Sprinkle with water and bake for 45 minutes to 1 hour, or until golden. Cool pie before making syrup.

Syrup:
  2 cups sugar
  3 cups water
  1 piece lemon peel

❏ In a medium saucepan, bring all the syrup ingredients to a boil for 15 minutes. Remove the lemon. When the pie is cooled, spoon the hot syrup over the top of the pie slowly. Serve warm or cold.

Serves 12.

EASY CAKE
(Afkolo Keik)

1 cup unsalted butter
1½ cups sugar
4 eggs, separated
½ cup milk
1 teaspoon vanilla
2½ cups flour
2 teaspoons baking powder
½ cup cocoa
½ cup chopped walnuts

Preheat the oven to 350 degrees F.

❏ Combine the butter with the sugar and beat together until creamy. Add the egg yolks, milk and vanilla. Beat all together into a creamy mixture.

❏ In a separate bowl, with clean beaters, beat the egg whites into stiff peaks. Set aside. Add the flour, baking powder and egg whites alternately to butter mixture. Blend these together to a smooth consistency.

❏ Grease a tube pan (bundt) and pour half the batter in. Mix walnuts and cocoa and arrange evenly over the batter. Add the remaining batter on top to cover the cocoa and walnuts.

❏ Bake for 45 minutes or until golden brown. Delicious.

Serves 12.

FINIKIA HOLIDAY COOKIES
(Finikia)

A most delicious treat for the holidays.

¾ cup unsalted butter
1 cup vegetable oil
¾ cup sugar
2 eggs
1 teaspoon vanilla
¾ cup fresh orange juice
5 to 6 cups flour
2 teaspoons baking powder
1 tablespoon ground cinnamon
1 tablespoon ground cloves
1½ tablespoons grated orange peel
¾ cup finely chopped walnuts mixed with 1
    tablespoon cinnamon for topping

Preheat the oven to 350 degrees F.

❑ In a large bowl, beat the butter with the oil until creamy. Add the sugar, eggs, vanilla and orange juice. Beat all together for 15 minutes. Mix the flour, baking powder, cinnamon, cloves, and orange peel. Add to the butter mixture. Mix together with your hands to form a soft but not stiff dough. Cover and let stand for 30 minutes. Form 1½ tablespoons into a cylinder and place on a cookie sheet about 1 inch apart. Bake for 25 to 30 minutes or until golden brown. Remove from the oven and let cool for 20 minutes.

Syrup:
  2 cups sugar
  3 cups water
  1 cup honey
  1 slice orange peel
  1 stick cinnamon

❑ In a medium saucepan, mix all the syrup ingredients. Boil for 15 minutes. Remove the orange peel and cinnamon. Lower the heat. With a slotted spoon, dip 4 to 5 cookies at a time into the hot syrup. Place cookies on large platter and sprinkle with the walnut and cinnamon mixture.

  Makes 4 dozen cookies.

GRANDMOTHER'S PASTRY HALVA
(Yiayias Halvas)

2½ cups sugar
1 slice lemon
1 cup unsalted butter
2 cups farina semolina
1½ cups roasted chopped almonds
1 teaspoon vanilla
1 teaspoon ground cinnamon
1 teaspoon ground cloves

❑ In a medium-size pot, combine 2 cups sugar, 3½ cups water and the lemon slice. Boil for 10 minutes. Melt the butter in a large saucepan until it is very hot, but do not let it brown. To the hot butter, add the farina and 1 cup of almonds, stirring slowly and constantly. Add the vanilla. Slowly add the hot syrup to the farina mixture while stirring constantly until it is thick. Remove from the heat and place a damp towel on top of this pan for at least 5 minutes. Spread the mixture evenly into a glass 9 x 13 x 2½ inch baking pan and sprinkle cinnamon, cloves, remaining ½ cup sugar and ½ cup almonds on the top. Lightly press almonds in with your palm and cut pastry into diamond-shaped serving pieces.

Let cool at room temperature and serve.

Serves 24.

HONEY YEAST BALLS
(Loukoumathes)

1 yeast cake, or 2 packages active dry yeast
2½ cups flour
1 teaspoon salt
1 to 1½ quarts vegetable oil
1 tablespoon ground cinnamon
½ cup finely chopped walnuts

Syrup:
   1 cup water
   1 cup honey
   1 cup sugar
   1 cinnamon stick

❏ In a large bowl, crumble the yeast and dissolve in 1½ cups of warm water. Stir in 1 cup of flour; cover bowl with a heavy towel and allow it to rise for 20 minutes. Then stir in 1½ cups of warm water, rest of flour, 1 teaspoon salt; cover and allow this to rise for 2 hours. When the dough is doubled in size, heat oil in a deep frying pan until very hot. Drop dough by tablespoons into the hot oil. (Dough will slide off spoon easily if you dip spoon in water before you take each spoonful of dough). Repeat this process until all the dough is used. Fry balls until they are golden brown in color. They will bubble up to the surface when they are done. Drain on a paper towel.

❏ Syrup: Mix all the syrup ingredients together and slowly boil for 15 minutes. This syrup must be thick. Remove the cinnamon stick. Place the loukoumathes on a platter and slowly pour the syrup over them. Lightly sprinkle with cinnamon and finely chopped walnuts.

Makes about 3 dozen.

MAMA'S CAKE
(Tis Mamas to Keik)

6 eggs
1½ cups sugar
1 cup unsalted butter, melted
¾ cup warm milk
1 teaspoon vanilla
3 cups flour
2 tablespoons baking powder
1 can (16 ounces) peaches, drained and chopped

Preheat the oven to 350 degrees F.

❏ In a large bowl, cream the eggs and sugar. Add the butter, milk and vanilla and beat for 5 minutes. Mix the flour, baking powder and peaches and add this to the egg mixture. Beat all together for 2 to 3 minutes.

❏ Grease and flour a tube pan (bundt) and pour this mixture evenly in and around the pan. Bake for 45 minutes to 1 hour or until golden brown. Allow to cool before serving.

Serves 12.

PASTRY ROLL WITH FILLO DOUGH
(Rolo Gemisto Me Fillo)

3 cups coarsely chopped walnuts
¼ cup dried bread crumbs
3 eggs
½ cup sugar
¼ cup fresh orange juice
1 teaspoon vanilla
1 pound fillo dough
½ cup unsalted butter, melted

Preheat the oven to 350 F.

❑ Combine the walnuts and bread crumbs in a large bowl and set aside. In a separate bowl, combine the eggs, sugar, orange juice and vanilla. Whip together for 3 to 4 minutes, then add to the walnut mixture and mix well. Take 2 fillo leaves and brush each one with butter and stack them. Put some walnut mixture in the middle of one short edge. Fold the two long sides in over the filling. Roll up. Repeat until all the mixture and fillo leaves are used. Brush an 18 x 12 inch jelly roll pan with butter. Cut each roll into 3 to 4 pieces and place on pan one inch apart; brush butter on top of each one. Sprinkle with water and bake for 30 to 35 minutes or until golden brown. Cool the pastries before making the syrup.

Syrup:
   2 cups sugar
   3 cups water
   ½ cup honey
   1 slice lemon
   1 stick cinnamon

❑ Mix all the syrup ingredients together in a saucepan. Boil for 10 to 15 minutes. Remove the lemon and cinnamon. Dip each pastry with a fork into the hot syrup and arrange on a platter. After you finish dipping all the pastries, boil the remaining syrup 2 to 3 minutes and pour it over the pastries. Allow them to cool and absorb the syrup for 5 to 6 hours before serving.

   Serves 24.

CAKE WITH COCONUT
(Keik Me Indokarido)

1 cup unsalted butter, melted
1 cup sugar
6 eggs
½ cup milk
1 teaspoon vanilla
3 cups flour
1 tablespoon baking powder
1 cup shredded coconut
1 teaspoon grated lemon peel

Preheat the oven to 350 degrees F.

❑ In a large bowl, beat the butter and sugar until creamy. Add the eggs, milk and vanilla and beat together for 10 minutes more. Mix the flour with the baking powder, coconut and lemon peel. Add this to the butter mixture slowly. Beat all together for 5 minutes.

❑ Grease a 9 x 13 inch pan. Pour the batter evenly into the pan and bake for 45 minutes to 1 hour. Make the syrup while the cake bakes.

Syrup:
2 cups sugar
3 cups water
2 teaspoons lemon juice
1 lemon peel, sliced

❑ Mix all the syrup ingredients and boil for 15 minutes. Cool completely. Allow the cake to cool for 5 minutes and slowly pour the cold syrup on top. Let stand for 3 to 4 hours before serving.

Makes 12 to 16.

REVANI CAKE WITH SYRUP
(Revani Me Siropi)

1½ cups flour
1 tablespoon baking powder
1 cup farina semolina
1 cup unsalted butter, melted
1 cup sugar
6 eggs, separated
1 tablespoon grated lemon
1 teaspoon vanilla
1 cup chopped roasted almonds

Preheat the oven to 350 degrees F.

❑ Mix the flour, baking powder and farina and set aside. In a large bowl, beat the butter and sugar until creamy. Add the egg yolks, lemon and vanilla. Beat all together. In a separate bowl, with clean beaters, beat the egg whites until they are stiff. Alternately add the egg whites, flour and farina, and almonds to the butter mixture, making sure they are well blended. Pour the batter into a greased 9 x 13 x 2½ inch pan and bake for 45 minutes to 1 hour, or until golden brown. Don't make the syrup until the cake has cooled for at least 45 minutes.

Syrup:
    2 cups sugar
    3 cups water
    1 piece lemon peel

❑ In a medium saucepan, boil all the syrup ingredients for 15 minutes. When the cake is cooled, cut into diamond-shaped pieces with a sharp knife. Slowly spoon the hot syrup all over the top. Let it stand for 3 to 4 hours at room temperature.

Serves 12.

ROX COFFEE COOKIES
(Rox)

¾ cup unsalted butter
1½ cups sugar
4 eggs
1 cup plain yogurt
1 tablespoon grated lemon peel
1 teaspoon vanilla
4 to 5 cups flour
1 tablespoon baking powder
1 cup chopped walnuts
1 cup raisins

Preheat the oven to 350 degrees F.

❑ In a large bowl, beat the butter, sugar and eggs until creamy. Add the yogurt, lemon peel and vanilla. Beat for 5 minutes. In a separate bowl, mix the flour, baking powder, walnuts and raisins. Add to the butter mixture until all ingredients are well blended. Knead gently with your hands until it forms a soft dough. Grease a cookie sheet and pinch off a tablespoon of dough per cookie. Roll into balls and place them an inch apart and bake for 20 to 25 minutes. Let cool.

Makes 3 dozen.

SHREDDED FILLO
(Kataifi)

3 cups chopped walnuts
1 cup roasted almonds, chopped
¼ cup dried bread crumbs
1 teaspoon ground cinnamon
¼ cup sugar
1 teaspoon ground cloves
¼ cup fresh orange juice
1 teaspoon vanilla
1 cup melted unsalted butter
1 package (1 pound) kataifi dough

Preheat the oven to 350 degrees F.

❑ In a large bowl, mix the walnuts, almonds, bread crumbs, cinnamon and sugar, plus the cloves, orange juice, vanilla and ¼ cup melted butter. On a clean flat surface, pull apart strands of kataifi dough with your fingers. Put 1 tablespoon of the walnut mixture at the end of a piece and roll into a cylinder around the filling. (Start rolling tightly and gradually loosen as you reach the end.) Continue this until you use up all of the filling and the kataifi dough. Place rolls 2 inches apart on a greased cookie sheet and brush with melted butter. Bake for 35 minutes or until golden brown. Make the syrup while the kataifi bakes.

Syrup:
  3 cups sugar
  4 cups water
  ½ cup honey
  2 whole cloves
  1 tablespoon lemon juice

❑ Mix together all the syrup ingredients and boil for 15 minutes. Take the kataifi out of the oven, let stand 10 minutes and spoon the hot syrup on top. Cover with a towel and let rest 6 to 8 hours before serving.

  Serves 24.

  Kataifi fillo dough may be purchased at Greek or Mediterranean markets.

TRADITIONAL EASTER TWIST COOKIES
(Pasxalina Koulourgia)

1½ pounds (6 sticks) unsalted butter
1½ cups sugar
6 eggs
1 tablespoon vanilla
¼ cup fresh orange juice
5 to 6 cups flour
4 teaspoons baking powder

Preheat the oven to 350 degrees F.

❏ Beat the butter and sugar in a large bowl until creamy. Add the eggs, vanilla, and orange juice and beat for 10 minutes. Mix the flour and baking powder and slowly add to the egg mixture. Knead with your hands to form a large ball. It should have a soft consistency. Let it stand for 30 minutes. Pinch off a piece of dough about the size of 1½ tablespoons and roll into a 5 inch rope. Fold rope in half and twist together. Place on a greased cookie sheet and brush top with egg wash. Place the cookies 1 inch apart. Bake for 20 to 25 minutes or until golden brown.

Makes 4 dozen.

WALNUT CAKE
(karithopita)

6 eggs, separated
¾ cup sugar
¼ cup fresh orange juice
¾ cup unsalted, melted butter
1 teaspoon vanilla
2 cups flour
1 tablespoon ground cinnamon
2 teaspoons baking powder
1 teaspoon ground cloves
1½ cups coarsely chopped walnuts
maraschino cherries, optional

Preheat the oven to 350 degrees F.

❏ In a large bowl, mix the egg yolks and sugar. Beat to a creamy consistency. Add the orange juice, butter and vanilla and beat all together for 5 minutes. In a separate bowl, with clean beaters, beat the egg whites until they form stiff peaks. Mix the flour, cinnamon, baking powder, cloves and walnuts together. Set aside. Alternately add the egg whites and the flour mixture to the egg and sugar batter until blended thoroughly. Grease a 9 x 13 x 2½ inch pan and pour the batter in evenly. Bake for 45 minutes to 1 hour. Allow to cool. Then, with a sharp knife, while still in the pan, cut into diamond-shaped pieces. Make the syrup after the cake has cooled.

Syrup:
  2 cups sugar
  3 cups water
  1 slice lemon
  1 teaspoon lemon juice
  1 stick cinnamon

❑ In a medium saucepan, boil all the syrup ingredients together for 15 minutes. Remove the cinnamon stick. Spoon the hot syrup slowly on top of the cake. If you wish, place a cherry on top of each piece. Cool in the pan for at least 4 to 5 hours.

  Serves 12.

YOGURT CAKE
(Keik Me Yiourti)

This delicious yogurt cake will satisfy your taste buds and stomach.

3 cups flour
1 tablespoon baking powder
1 tablespoon grated lemon peel
6 eggs, separated
1½ cups sugar
1 cup unsalted, melted butter
1 cup plain yogurt
1 cup chopped blanched toasted almonds
1 teaspoon vanilla

Preheat the oven to 350 degrees F.

❑ Mix the flour, baking powder and lemon peel in a bowl. Set aside. In a large bowl, beat the egg yolks and sugar together until creamy. Add the butter, yogurt and vanilla and beat for 10 minutes. In a separate bowl, with clean beaters, beat the egg whites until stiff peaks form. Alternately fold the almonds, egg whites and flour into the egg yolk mixture. Grease and lightly flour a tube pan (bundt). Pour the cake mixture evenly around the tube. Bake for 1 hour and allow the cake to cool before serving.

Serves 8.

MEZEDES (APPETIZERS)
and
OTHER FAVORITES

ARTICHOKE SALAD
(Aginares Salata)

2 cans (14 ounces each) artichokes hearts, drained
2 medium tomatoes, sliced
1 medium cucumber, sliced
1 tablespoon finely chopped fresh parsley
¼ cup olive oil
juice of 1 lemon
2 cloves garlic, crushed
½ teaspoon dry oregano
½ teaspoon dry thyme
salt and pepper

❏ Cut artichokes in half and arrange on a platter. Arrange the tomatoes and cucumber around the artichokes, and sprinkle the salad with parsley.

❏ To make the dressing, combine the oil, lemon juice, garlic, oregano, thyme, and salt and pepper to taste, and mix well. Pour the dressing over the vegetables on the platter.

Serves 4.

CABBAGE SALAD
(Lahanosalata)

½ pound green cabbage, shredded
2 medium carrots, shredded
1 tablespoon chopped fresh parsley plus additional for
    garnish
10 Kalamata olives
juice of 1 lemon
¼ cup olive oil
1 teaspoon honey
salt

❑ Place the cabbage in the bottom of a large salad bowl. Layer the carrots over the cabbage, and sprinkle with parsley and olives.

❑ To make the dressing, combine the lemon juice, olive oil, honey, and salt to taste. Mix well and pour the dressing over the cabbage and carrots. Sprinkle with additional parsley for garnish.

Serves 4 to 5.

TOMATO SALAD
(Tomatosalata)

Olive oil is the only dressing needed for this salad, which is delicious served with fresh crusty bread.

3 to 4 ripe tomatoes, sliced
1 medium Italian sweet pepper, sliced
1 small onion, thinly sliced
¾ cup feta cheese, crumbled
½ teaspoon dry oregano
salt and pepper
¼ cup olive oil

❑ Place the ingredients in a large salad bowl in the following order: tomatoes, pepper, onion, and feta. Sprinkle with oregano, salt and pepper to taste, and olive oil.

Serves 3 to 4.

COUNTRY SALAD
(Horiatikh Salata)

1 head Romaine lettuce, washed and chopped
2 tomatoes, sliced
1 cucumber, sliced
½ cup sliced green onions
1 tablespoon chopped fresh dill
1 Italian sweet pepper, sliced in round pieces
½ cup feta cheese, cut into cubes
10 Kalamata olives

Dressing:
¼ cup olive oil
juice of 1 lemon
salt and pepper
½ teaspoon dry oregano

❏ Place the ingredients into a large salad bowl in the following order: lettuce, tomatoes, cucumbers, green onions, dill, peppers, feta, and olives.

❏ To make the dressing: in a small container, combine oil, lemon juice, salt and pepper to taste, and oregano. Mix well and pour it over the salad.

Serves 4.

FRIED CHEESE
(Saganaki)

Saganaki is one of the best-loved mezze in the Greek culture. Serve this hearty appetizer with ouzo and bread.

¾ pound kefalotyri cheese (or any hard yellow cheese)
juice of 1 lemon
½ cup flour
½ teaspoon dry oregano
½ teaspoon dry mint
½ teaspoon paprika
freshly ground pepper to taste
½ cup olive oil
1 tablespoon chopped fresh parsley

❑ Cut cheese into wedges about 3 inches long and ¾-inch thick. Place the cheese wedges on a platter and sprinkle with the lemon juice. In a medium bowl combine the flour, oregano, mint, paprika, and ground pepper, and then dredge cheese lightly in flour mixture. Heat oil in a heavy skillet. Add a few pieces of cheese at a time and flip to fry on both sides about 3 to 4 minutes or until golden brown. Sprinkle with chopped parsley.

Serves 4.

RICE PILAF WITH MUSHROOMS
(Pilafi Me Manitaria)

¼ cup olive oil
1 cup chopped onions
3 cloves garlic, crushed
1 ½ cups sliced fresh mushrooms
1 medium red pepper, chopped
2 cups long-grain rice
4 cups chicken broth
2 bay leaves
1 ½ teaspoons dry mint
salt and pepper

❑ In a medium saucepan heat oil and sauté onions, garlic, mushrooms, and pepper for 5 minutes. Then add rice, stir over heat for 1 minute, and then add chicken broth, bay leaves, mint, and salt and pepper to taste. Stir and allow the rice to cook on high for 10 minutes. Lower the heat and cover until the liquid is absorbed, and the rice is soft, about 15 minutes. Remove from the heat.

❑ Serve hot as a side dish with chicken, meat or fish.

Serves 6.

PIZZA BREAD APPETIZER
(Psomi Oregtiko)

3 to 3½ cups all-purpose flour
2 teaspoons baking powder
1 teaspoon salt
1 cup water
1 cup chopped Kalamata olives
2 tablespoons olive oil
½ cup finely chopped green onion (white parts only)
3 garlic cloves, finely chopped
2 tablespoons finely chopped parsley
1 tablespoon finely chopped mint
½ teaspoon dry oregano
½ cup grated kefalotyri cheese or Parmesan cheese

❑ In a large bowl sift flour, baking powder, and salt. Make a well in the center. Add water, olives, olive oil, green onions, garlic, parsley, mint, oregano, and cheese. Stir all the ingredients with a fork until dough is formed. Then turn dough onto a lightly floured surface. Knead until dough is smooth (about 10 minutes). Add more flour if dough begins to stick to your hands. Cover the dough and let stand for 1 hour.

❑ Preheat oven to 375 degrees F. Lightly brush a pizza pan with olive oil, and then shape dough into a ball and press down gently with your palms to fit evenly into the pizza pan. Bake for 50 minutes to 1 hour until golden brown on top. Remove from the oven and let stand for 10 minutes. Remove from the pan and cut to diamond-shape pieces.

❏ Arrange pita triangles on a platter and serve with feta cheese spread.

Serves 4.

KALAMATA OLIVE DIP
(Elies Kopanistes)

This delicious dip can be served with crusty bread or pita bread.

    1 pound Kalamata olives
    1 onion, chopped
    3 garlic cloves, chopped
    1 tablespoon chopped fresh mint
    juice of 1 lemon
    1 teaspoon dry oregano
    ½ teaspoon dry basil
    additional chopped mint or parsley for garnish

❑ Rinse the olives 2 to 3 times in water, drain, and pit them. Combine olives, onion, garlic, mint, lemon juice, oregano, and basil in a food processor or blender. Blend the mixture for 2 to 3 minutes or until it becomes a smooth paste. Place the dip in a medium-size bowl and garnish with chopped mint or parsley. Cover and refrigerate. This dip will keep in the refrigerator for 4 to 5 days.

Yields 1¼ cups.

MARINATED OLIVES
(Elies Horiatikes)

This delicious recipe comes straight from my mom's kitchen.

1 pound Kalamata or green Greek olives
3 to 4 garlic cloves, crushed
1 teaspoon chopped fresh rosemary
1 teaspoon dry oregano
1½ teaspoons chopped fresh thyme
1 bay leaf, crushed
1 lemon, sliced
½ cup red wine vinegar
½ cup olive oil

❑ Place olives into a colander and rinse with cold water 2 to 3 times. Let the water drain and place the olives in a large bowl. In a medium bowl, combine the garlic, rosemary, oregano, thyme, bay leaf, lemon slices, vinegar, and olive oil. Mix well. Pour the vinegar-oil mixture over the olives and mix well. Place the marinated olives in a large jar, cover, and refrigerate 4 to 5 days before serving as an appetizer.

Serves 6.

SPICED FETA APPETIZER
(Mezethaki me tyrl feta)

1 pound feta cheese
1 teaspoon dry oregano
1 tablespoon chopped fresh thyme
3 cloves garlic, finely chopped
juice of ½ a lemon
½ cup olive oil
freshly ground black pepper

❑ Rinse the feta with cold water and pat dry. Cut the feta into large cubes and place in a bowl. In small jar, mix oregano, thyme, garlic, lemon juice, olive oil, and pepper. Pour the oil over the feta. Cover and refrigerate at least 1 to 2 weeks. Serve the marinated feta as an appetizer with crusty bread. It is also delicious with ouzo.

Serves 6.

FETA CHEESE TRIANGLES
(Tiropitakia)

½ pound feta cheese, crumbled
¼ pound farmer cheese
¼ cup grated Parmesan cheese
1½ tablespoons finely chopped fresh mint
½ teaspoon nutmeg
2 eggs, beaten
1 tablespoon olive oil plus ¼ cup for brushing fillo
fresh ground pepper
salt (to taste, depending on the saltiness of the feta cheese)
1 pound fillo dough

❏ In a large bowl combine feta cheese, farmer cheese, Parmesan, mint, nutmeg, eggs, 1 tablespoon olive oil, and fresh pepper. Blend very well with a fork. Cover and refrigerate for 35 minutes.

❏ Preheat oven to 350 degrees F.

❏ Pour the ¼ cup olive oil for brushing the fillo into a small bowl. Unroll fillo dough and keep covered while working with 2 sheets at a time. Cut each fillo sheet into 4 long strips. Brush each strip with olive oil and place 1 tablespoon of the cheese filling in the middle bottom of each strip. Fold right corner up and to the left, to form a right angle. Repeat the same steps for remaining fillo and filling. Place cheese triangles on a greased cookie sheet 1 inch apart. Brush top with oil and sprinkle with a little water. Bake about 20 to 25 minutes or until golden brown. Serve hot or cold.

Yields 2½ to 3 dozen triangles.

FETA CHEESE OMELET
(Omeleta me Feta)

This is my favorite omelet recipe.

3 tablespoons olive oil
4 eggs
2 tablespoons milk
½ cup crumbled feta cheese
1 tablespoon grated Parmesan
1 tablespoon finely chopped parsley
salt and ground pepper

❏ Heat the olive oil in a medium-size skillet. In small bowl beat eggs, add milk, feta, Parmesan, parsley, and salt and pepper to taste. Beat all the ingredients together for 1 minute. Pour the egg mixture into hot oil and cook for 2 to 3 minutes until omelet sets. Flip omelet and cook until both sides are golden brown.

Serves 2.

SCRAMBLED EGG OMELET
WITH TOMATOES
(Kayianas)

This delicious omelet is from my hometown Amaliada No-mos Elias in Peloponnese. It can be served for either lunch or dinner.

1 tablespoon olive oil
1 medium onion, finely chopped
1 large Italian sweet pepper, sliced into rounds
3 medium tomatoes, skinned and chopped
6 eggs
½ cup crumbled feta cheese
salt and pepper
1 tablespoon finely chopped parsley for garnish

❑ In a large skillet, heat the olive oil and add the onion. Sauté for 2 to 3 minutes until the onion is soft and then add the peppers. Stir and sauté for 2 to 3 minutes. Add the tomatoes and simmer for 5 minutes. In a medium bowl beat the eggs with the cheese. Add salt and pepper to taste. Pour egg mixture into skillet and stir with wooden spoon for 5 to 6 minutes.
Serve hot and sprinkled with parsley.

Serves 3.

GRILLED LAMB SOUDZOUKAKIA ON SKEWERS
(Soudzoukakia Souvlaki)

1½ to 2 pounds lean ground lamb
1 medium onion, finely chopped
3 cloves garlic, finely chopped
1 tablespoon finely chopped mint
1 teaspoon dry oregano
½ teaspoon ground cumin
2 tablespoons finely chopped parsley
¼ cup plain bread crumbs
1 egg, beaten
1 tablespoon lemon juice
salt and pepper
skewers

❑ In a large bowl knead together the ground lamb, onions, garlic, mint, oregano, cumin, parsley, bread crumbs, egg, lemon juice, and salt and pepper to taste. Combine the ingredients well by hand, cover, and refrigerate for 1 hour.

❑ Preheat grill or prepare for grilling. Dampen your hands with a little oil, take an egg-size handful of the meat mixture, and shape it into a long thin sausage. Place a skewer through the length of the sausage and continue this process until all the meat mixture is used. Grill the *soudzoukakia* for 8 to 10 minutes, turning them from time to time.

❑ Serve hot with Greek salad, rice pilaf, warm pita bread and Tzadziki Sauce (see page 69). This dish also makes a delicious sandwich (similar to gyros) with pita bread, tomatoes, onions, lettuce, and tzadziki sauce.

Serves 4 to 5.

GRILLED LAMB HAMBURGER PATTIES WITH FETA CHEESE
(Bifteki me- feta)

This recipe makes a unique and delicious "Greek" version of the classic hamburger.

1½ pounds lean ground lamb
1 large onion, grated
2 cloves garlic, finely chopped
1 tablespoon finely chopped fresh mint
1 teaspoon dry oregano
¼ cup plain bread crumbs
2 tablespoons lemon juice
salt and pepper
4 to 5 hamburger buns
1 tablespoon olive oil
½ pound feta cheese, sliced
1 onion, sliced round
1 tomato, sliced
1 to 1½ cups shredded iceberg lettuce

Preheat the grill or prepare for grilling.

❑ In a large bowl combine the lamb with the onion, garlic, mint, oregano, bread crumbs, lemon juice, and salt and pepper to taste. Knead with your hands to mix all ingredients together. Form the meat mixture into 4 to 5 patties and set aside. Grill each patty for 6 to 7 minutes on each side for medium rare or until desired doneness. Brush hamburger buns with oil, place on the rack cut side down, and grill until golden brown. Place each burger on the bottom half of the toasted bun and top with slice of the feta cheese, onions, tomatoes, and lettuce, and cover with the top bun. Serve hot with homemade French fried potatoes.

Serves 4.

CHICKEN TRIANGLES WITH BÉCHAMEL SAUCE
(Kotopitakia me béchamel)

3 tablespoons olive oil
1 medium onion, grated
1 medium red pepper, finely chopped
2 cloves garlic, crushed
1 tablespoon fresh chopped parsley
1½ to 2 pounds chicken breast, cut into very small
  pieces
1 teaspoon dry oregano
½ teaspoon dry mint
¼ cup white wine
salt and pepper

Béchamel Sauce:
1½ tablespoons butter
2 tablespoons flour
1 cup warm milk
2 eggs yolks
½ cup grated kefalotyri or Romano cheese
pinch of nutmeg

1 pound fillo dough
¼ cup olive oil or butter

Chicken Mixture:
❑ Heat oil in a large skillet and add onion, peppers, garlic, and parsley. Sauté until lightly brown. Add chicken breast pieces, oregano, mint, wine, and salt and pepper to taste. Stir well. Reduce the heat to medium low and

let simmer for 15 to 20 minutes. Remove from the heat. Place the mixture into a large bowl.

Béchamel Sauce:
❏ Melt the butter in a small saucepan and add the flour. Continue stirring, slowly adding milk and stirring for a smooth and creamy consistency. Remove from the heat. In medium bowl beat the egg yolks with a fork. Add the eggs yolks to the milk mixture with cheese and nutmeg and stir all together very well.

❏ Preheat the oven to 350 degrees F. Add béchamel sauce to the chicken mixture, and combine well. Take 1 to 1½ teaspoons of the mixture for each triangle and fold with fillo dough according to the same directions as "Feta Cheese Triangles" page 185. Brush each triangle with oil or butter and place folded side down on the cookie sheet and bake for 15 to 20 minutes or until golden brown. Serve hot.

Serves 2.

GRECIAN GRILLED CHICKEN BREASTS
(Kota Stithos Sta Karvouna)

2 whole chicken breasts, each cut in half
¼ cup olive oil
juice of 1 lemon
1 tablespoon honey
1 teaspoon dry oregano
½ teaspoon dry thyme
3 cloves garlic, crushed
1 teaspoon mustard
1 bay leaf, crushed
salt and pepper

❑ Wash and pat dry chicken breasts. In a large bowl whisk together the olive oil, lemon juice, honey, oregano, thyme, garlic, mustard, bay leaf, and salt and pepper to taste. Cover and refrigerate about 3 to 4 hours, turning the chicken once in between to allow it to marinate on both sides.

❑ Preheat grill or prepare for grilling. Remove the chicken breasts from the marinade and place on the hot grill. Cook for 10 minutes on each side or until chicken is tender.

Served hot with rice pilaf, tomato salad and hot pita bread. This dish is also delicious with Tzadziki Sauce (page 69).

Serves 4.

STUFFED CHICKEN BREAST
WITH FETA CHEESE
(Kota stithos Gemisto Me Feta)

3 whole chicken breasts, each cut in half
juice of 2 lemons
salt and pepper
3 cloves garlic, crushed
1 teaspoon oregano
2 tablespoons finely chopped parsley
6 slices ham
½ pound feta cheese, sliced
3 tablespoons olive oil
½ teaspoon dry thyme
½ cup plain bread crumbs
1 teaspoon paprika

Preheat oven to 350 degrees F.

❏ Wash and pat dry the chicken breasts. Pound each chicken breast until it is thin. Then place them on a large platter, sprinkle with the juice of 1 lemon, and salt and pepper to taste. Rub the chicken breast with the crushed garlic, and sprinkle with oregano and parsley. Start by placing a slice of ham on the top of the chicken breast then place a slice of feta cheese on top of the ham. Roll chicken breast and secure with toothpick. In a medium bowl, beat oil, juice of the remaining lemon, thyme, and additional salt and pepper. Place the chicken rolls in baking pan 1 inch apart and brush with oil mixture and sprinkle with bread crumbs and paprika. Add ½ cup water to the bottom of the pan. Bake for 45 to 50 minutes or until chicken rolls are tender. Remove from oven and let them cool for 5 minutes. Serve with rice and any greens or salad.

Serves 6.

GRILLED PORK CHOPS
(Paithakia Sta Karvouna)

6 pork chops (with bones), trimmed of fat
¼ cup olive oil
juice of 1½ lemons
3 cloves garlic, minced
1 teaspoon finely chopped fresh rosemary
1 teaspoon dry oregano
1 teaspoon dry thyme
salt and pepper
lemon wedges

❑ Wash and pat dry the pork chops, and place in a large bowl. In a medium bowl, whisk together olive oil, lemon juice, garlic, rosemary, oregano, thyme, and salt and pepper to taste. Pour olive oil marinade over the pork chops and turn 2 to 3 times to coat thoroughly. Cover and refrigerate about 4 to 6 hours.

❑ Preheat the grill or prepare for grilling. Remove the chops from the marinade and place onto hot grill. Cook for 6 to 8 minutes. Turn over one more time and cook for a final 2 to 3 minutes for medium rare or longer for desired doneness. Serve hot, garnished with lemon wedges.

Serves 6.

STUFFED SAUSAGE WITH FETA IN FILLO ROLLS
(Loukaniko rollo-me-fillo)

6 Greek loukaniko or any type of sweet Italian sausages
½ pound feta cheese, cut into long strips
¼ cup finely chopped parsley
6 sheets fillo dough
¼ cup olive oil

Preheat the oven to 350 degrees F.

❑ Pierce the sausages with a fork, place in a large skillet over medium heat, and brown on both sides. Remove and pat dry with paper towels. With a sharp knife make a slit (3 inches lengthwise) in each sausage. Insert a strip of feta cheese in each slit. Sprinkle with parsley.

❑ Take 1 fillo sheet and brush with oil. Place sausage in the middle and fold over placing both sides (left and right) inwards and then roll it up. Repeat with remaining fillo sheets. Brush each pastry with oil and place on a cookie sheet 1 inch apart from each other. Score the top into 1½ to 2 inches. Do not cut all the way down. Brush with more oil and sprinkle with water. Bake for 25 to 30 minutes or until golden brown. Remove from the oven and let cool for 25 to 30 minutes. Cut sausage rolls into complete pieces following the pattern of the scoring. Place the sausages on a platter and garnish with parsley sprigs. These rolls are a delicious appetizer or first course with wine or ouzo.

Serves 6.

GRILLED RED SNAPPER
(Synagritha Sta Karvouna)

1 or 2 whole red snappers (about 1½ to 2 pounds)
juice of 1 lemon
salt and pepper
1 teaspoon dry oregano
3 cloves garlic, minced
2 tablespoons olive oil
4 fresh parsley springs
2 bay leaves
lemon slices

Preheat grill or prepare for grilling.

❑ Clean fish and pat dry. Make 3 diagonal slashes on each side. Sprinkle with lemon juice, salt and pepper to taste, oregano, and garlic, both inside and outside the fish. Tear off a piece of aluminum foil large enough to enclose fish. Brush a little oil on the side of the foil that the fish is lying on. Place parsley and bay leaves in the fish cavity and sprinkle remaining oil on top of fish. Wrap foil around the fish and fold the edges over to seal.

❑ Cook the fish on top of the grill for about 20 to 30 minutes or until tender. Test during cooking by inserting a toothpick into thickest part of the fish; if the flesh is tender and white, the fish is done. Serve with lemon slices.

Serves 2 to 3.

BAKED FISH PLAKI
(Psari Plaki-sto- fourno)

1 to 1½ pounds fish fillets (haddock, cod, or red
   snapper)
juice of 1 lemon
¼ cup olive oil
2 large onions, thinly sliced
3 cloves garlic, minced
¼ cup chopped fresh parsley
2 tablespoons chopped fresh mint
½ cup white wine
1 cup chopped peeled tomatoes
1 teaspoon dry oregano
salt and pepper
2 tablespoons plain bread crumbs
lemon slices

Preheat the oven to 350 degrees F.

❑ Wash the fish and cut it into pieces. Place the fish on a
platter and sprinkle with lemon juice on top. Cover and
set aside while preparing the sauce. In a large skillet,
heat olive oil and sauté onion and garlic for 2 to 3
minutes. Add parsley and mint and sauté for 2 more
minutes; add wine, tomatoes, oregano, and salt and
pepper to taste. Reduce heat to medium-low, cover, and
simmer for 10 to 15 minutes until most of the liquid
evaporates. Remove from the heat.

❑ Spoon some of the sauce onto the bottom of medium-
size pan, arrange fish over it, and top with the remaining
sauce. Sprinkle with bread crumbs and bake for 45

minutes or until fish is tender. Baste the fish with sauce a few times during cooking. Remove from the oven. Serve hot. Garnish with lemon slices and additional chopped parsley.

Serves 4.

MUSSELS WITH WINE
(Mythial Me Krasi)

This elegant dish makes a delicious appetizer or first course.

2½ to 3 pounds mussels
¼ cup olive oil
1 large onion, grated
4 garlic cloves, finely chopped
1 sweet red pepper, chopped
1 cup white wine
2 bay leaves
1 cinnamon stick
1 teaspoon oregano
salt and pepper
2 tablespoons finely chopped parsley

❑ Scrub the shells of the mussels with a hard brush and scrape off any debris. Debeard them and rinse well with cold water. Heat olive oil in a large pot and sauté onion, garlic, and pepper for 5 minutes. Add mussels and stir all together for 5 more minutes. Add wine, bay leaves, cinnamon, oregano, and salt and pepper to taste. Sprinkle with chopped parsley, cover, and let cook for 10 to 15 minutes until mussels open. Discard any that do not open. Place the mussels in a large bowl with sauce. Serve hot with crusty bread and wine or ouzo.

Serves 5 to 6.

SHRIMP WITH FETA AND TOMATO SAUCE
(Garides Me Feta Kai Tomates)

¼ cup olive oil
1 large onion, chopped
3 cloves garlic, finely chopped
1 green pepper, chopped
2 tablespoons finely chopped parsley
3 ripe tomatoes, peeled and chopped
½ teaspoon dry oregano
1 bay leaf
½ teaspoon sugar
salt and pepper
1 to 1½ pounds medium shrimp, washed, deveined and shelled
½ pound feta cheese, sliced

Preheat the oven to 350 degrees F.

❑ In a large skillet, heat oil and sauté onion, garlic, pepper and parsley together for 5 minutes. Add the tomatoes, oregano, bay leaf, sugar, salt and pepper to taste, and ½ cup water. Reduce the heat to medium-low and simmer for 15 to 20 minutes. Add shrimp, stir, and cook for 5 minutes. Remove from the heat. Place the shrimp in a medium-size glass baking dish and top with feta slices. Bake for 15 minutes or until feta starts to melt. Remove from the oven let cool for 5 minutes. Serve with rice pilaf, salad, and bread.

Serves 4 to 5.

Index

Index

Note: (*) Recipes with an asterisk indicate that these are the popular basic Greek recipes.

MEZEDES (APPETIZERS) AND OTHER FAVORITES: